INTERNATIONAL TOURISM

INTERNATIONAL TOURISM

A Political and Social Analysis

Harry G. Matthews

SCHENKMAN PUBLISHING COMPANY
Cambridge, Massachusetts

For HARRIET —
My Favorite Tourist

Copyright © 1978

Schenkman Publishing Company, Inc.

Library of Congress Cataloging in Publication Data

Matthews, Harry G. 1939-
   International tourism
   Bibliography: p.
   1. Tourist trade. I. Title.
G155.A1M38   338.4′7′91   77-24764
ISBN 0-87073-944-1
ISBN 0-87073-945-X pbk.

Printed in the United States of America

ALL RIGHTS RESERVED. THIS BOOK, OR PARTS THEREOF, MAY NOT BE REPRODUCED IN ANY FORM WITHOUT WRITTEN PERMISSION OF THE PUBLISHER.

CONTENTS

Preface		vii
1. The Transnational Scene		3
The Nature of Mass Tourism	3	
Conceptual Framework	5	
The International Context	6	
Tourism and International Relations	9	
Some World View Critiques	13	
2. Tourism Politics in the Marketplace		16
Important Private Actors	17	
Travel Agents	18	
Airlines	21	
Other Tourism Lobbies	36	
The Metropolitan Government and Tourism	37	
3. The Developing Host Country		44
The Development Issue	45	
The Cultural Issue	50	
Clusters of Political Interest	52	
National Government	52	
Local Elites	58	
Populist Groups	61	
Labor Unions	61	
The Church	66	
Academics and Others	69	
4. Some Biased Perceptions of Tourism		74
Tourism and Capitalism	75	
Third World Perceptions	78	
As Neo-Colonialism and Neo-Imperialism	79	
As Plantation Economy	80	
As Playground Culture	81	
As White Intrusion	81	
As Fantasy	82	
5. Conclusion: System Politics and Tourism		87
A Systemic View of Tourism	91	
The Future and Tourism Politics	91	
Notes		
Suggested Readings		94
EPILOGUE		97

TABLES

Table No.		page
1.	Foreign Currency Earnings from International Tourism of Various Countries	7
2.	Tourists Arrivals by Region	7
3.	Selected OECD Countries: Tourism Earnings as % of Exports and Expenditure	8
4.	North Atlantic Air Passenger Traffic, 1973	8
5.	Directional Flow of American Travelers, 1973	17
6.	Receipts, Expenditures and Travel Balances of Various Metropolitan Countries, 1973	18
7.	North Atlantic Scheduled Passengers and Load Factors, By Carrier, 1974	28
8.	Numbers of Passengers Carried by U. S. In International Charter Flights, 1974	31
9.	Net Profits of U. S. Air Carriers, 1974	35
10.	Arrivals and Receipts from Six USTS Market Countries, 1974	38
11.	Ownership of Hotels in Barbados, By Type, 1971	47
12.	Wage Negotiations, Barbados Hotel Strike, 1974	62
13.	Selected Weekly Wage Rates, Luxury Hotels in Barbados, 1973 and 1975	63

ILLUSTRATIONS

A.	Major Interest Group Clusters: Tourism Politics in Developing Countries	53
B.	Barbados Government Tourism Poster	66
C.	Scantily Clad Tourist in Barbados	68
D.	Behavioral Science Dimensions of Tourism	88
E.	Political Relations in World Tourism	89
F.	Systems Model of Tourism Politics	92

PREFACE

For many years the Caribbean with its varieties of island nations and cultures has been a popular destination for millions of American travelers in search of tropical leisure. During those same years I, as a researcher and teacher of political science, have been in the same region seeking to learn more about politics in small states — about various links between the Caribbean and the rest of the world.

Over the years I have observed tourists and their behavior in different islands. As a guest in accommodations ranging from boarding houses to luxury hotels, I gradually became intrigued with tourism as a political link between common people in developing countries and in the societies of Europe and North America. There appeared everywhere in tourism the potential for friendship and serious conflict, both of which could easily be observed.

It was when I first studied the conflicts between Black Power and multinational corporations in the Caribbean that tourism first became fascinating to me. It became clear that corporate and other economic concerns dominated the industry. I discovered, much to my surprise or proving my naïvete, that in both the United States and in the Caribbean there are persons who fear that world tourism has become a force for conflict and the denial of nationhood in many Third and Fourth World countries.

This short book is reflective of a dual interest in the political conflicts in young nations of the Caribbean and in the role of transnational business in those conflicts. For the Caribbean tourism is a good case study of these two things.

I must thank a number of people and institutions either for time and cooperation or for financial support. Many costs were borne by Northern Arizona University and by the Transition Foundation of Los Angeles. In Barbados and the Caribbean numerous people were of great help: Frank Walcott and Lyn Greaves of the Barbados Workers Union; Peter Morgan, Minister of Tourism in Barbados; Rudolf Geiner and Rudolf Schouten with Hilton International Corporation; Raymond Yelle with Commonwealth Holiday Inns of Canada, Ltd.; and various persons connected with Barclay Bank, Bank of America, Eastern Airlines, British West

Indian Airways, and with the Barbados Hotel Association.

In the United States, cooperation and information were generously given by the Caribbean Tourism Association, U. S. Travel Service, the World Bank, Hilton Hotels, Inc., the National Air Carrier Association, the Air Transport Association, the Organization of American States, and others.

My deepest gratitude goes to Herbert Hiller. His intellectual and moral commitment to both tourism and the people it affects is surely an inspiration to anyone writing on the subject.

Harry G. Matthews

INTERNATIONAL TOURISM

1
THE TRANSNATIONAL SCENE

International tourism today must be described primarily as *mass* tourism — the movement of large numbers of travelers from one country to another by means of mass transport, and this involves mass hotel accommodations, and above all, mass selling. It is precisely this quality of modern tourism that makes the industry so complex and so highly political. The activity which we call tourism has become intensely institutionalized and competitive.

Tourism and International Relations

Today's international tourists, like flights of geese, reach their destinations by flying in formation. On long journeys they stay overnight at designated watering-holes which are located purposely at intervals of not more than a day's flight. The selection of these overnight sites, known in human circles as resorts (maybe geese have a *honk* for them), is not made by the individual goose, but rather by the lead-geese. In modern mass tourism there are scores of lead-geese: as examples, we can list one's friendly hometown travel agency, numerous airlines, hotel chains, the credit card companies, and even one's own government. The actions of all these *super-geese* can alter the pattern of world tourism by determining the relative convenience and costs of foreign vacations for the millions who may seek a respite from the winter's cold, or pleasant interruptions of the pace of industrial-urban life, or fun in the sun at one of the world's playgrounds. Modern tourists, like geese, seem to possess an instinctive drive to go south during the winter, adhering to major fly ways where the best holidays can be obtained for the least cost or travel time.

Although modern tourism can be a highly political act, the politics of international mass tourism has not been the subject of widespread study. Few social and behavioral scientists have taken advantage of this phenomenon as a means of studying international or national politics. Tourism is usually analyzed from a market perspective: who has what to sell and who wants to buy it? Information abounds describing how sunshine and sea water can be packaged with hotel and air fare and sold for profit; how *culture-bound* travelers can meet the people of foreign countries or how traveling to distant lands can be relaxing and educational at the same time. Special interest travelers such as educators, clergy, athletes, or musicians probably come closest to learning something about their destination culture. Yet, most institutions involved in mass tourism know much more about their clients — that is, the tourists — than they know about the host societies and the impact of tourism upon those societies. Certainly this situation prevails in those host nations who have only recently become aware of the tremendous potential which their fresh appeal extends to those who are forever seeking out new, exotic places to visit. For that reason, this study is not heavily concerned with the perennially popular tourist attractions such as European countries or Hawaii. Rather, it is limited to Barbados and the eastern Caribbean, which perhaps typify the many small and new nations of the world which are now trying to cope with the effects of mass tourism.

This study examines the politics of international tourism at three levels: it examines the metropolitan country wherein lies the market for tourism, the host "developing nation" where tourists go, and groups whose attitudes toward tourism are shaped primarily by their respective philosophies or ideologies. The main focus of this study is upon North America as a market place and upon the Caribbean as a host region. More specifically, the research has concentrated upon Canadian and American corporate intrusions into the eastern Caribbean. There, Barbados has achieved by far the most highly developed tourism industry and offers a good case study of the impact of international tourism upon a small host country. The effects of tourism upon political and social development are not the same for all countries. The level and kind of tourism which a nation allows to emerge depend on many factors. In many developing countries today international mass tourism is a reality; in many other regions it is a much sought-after industry.

Comparative sociologists more than others have begun to examine the problems of interaction between host populations and foreign visitors. Race relations, sexual mores, and changing values and tastes are logical subjects of sociological research. Too, economists have given some attention to the economic value of tourism. But where the sociologists and economists stop, political scientists must begin. Political and social development builds upon a synthesis of the society's strengths and weaknesses, upon its prominent values, institutions, hopes, and fears. These features must be reconciled not only to economic realities but also to the political realities in both developed and "developing" societies.

Mass tourism does not happen in a vacuum. Transnational actors — hotel and airline corporations — promote and facilitate the industry wherever a reasonable profit can be expected. In

Barbados, over 62% of the year's visitors to the island in 1974 were North Americans. The invasion by large numbers of metropolitan tourists was preceded by the establishment of corporate beach heads by airline routes, hotel construction, and arrays of consumer goods that make the visitor *feel at home.*

How does all this come about? What are the issues upon which governments must act in pursuit of the international tourism promoted by airlines, hotel chains, banks, and other related institutions? In what ways do the giants of the tourism industry lobby their own governments? How successful are they? What are the effects of all this upon the host society? Are North American rather than West Indian values becoming the measure of politics and development in Barbados What are the politics of tourism there?

Like the *politics of oil* or the *politics of the environment,* the *politics* of international tourism is a very important dimension of world tourism. Governmental decisions and efforts to affect those decisions are an important key to the growth and nature of world tourism. These decisions take place in different environments — in the metropolitan areas of the globe where most tourists reside, in the host countries which have sought a growing tourism industry, and in private groups which support or oppose governmental decisions affecting tourism.

In the final analysis some tough but essential questions must be asked: To what extent does international tourism contribute favorably to international relations and understanding? In what ways is it divisive of peoples and cultures? Is tourism, like the worldwide search for energy, an aggressive creation of industrial societies, pursuing leisure at the expense of the non-industrial countries? In the political processes of international tourism lie the answers to some of these questions.

Conceptual Framework. — There are several possible contexts in which this study could be conducted, but perhaps one is more fitting than the others. Since the research focuses upon the *politics* of tourism, quite logically a domestic-political approach in two systems is best. That is, the politics which give rise to international tourism will be studied in two environments: the metropolitan marketplace (the United States) and the receiving societies (Barbados and/or the eastern Caribbean). To the extent that actors and events in each of these systems give rise to international relations and international politics, then the transnational aspects of tourism politics must be included.

This means that interest group politics and pluralism will be the theoretical framework. (It will be desirable to identify the interest groups of international tourism in both the sending and receiving states, and to identify what their goals are, and how governments have responded to their demands.) There is, however, much more in tourism politics than group efforts to increase profits (in spite of government constraints). The idea of pluralism suggests that the very concept of tourism can be challenged by other interest groups — by groups whose concerns may be more ideological or moral than economic. As we shall see in subsequent chapters, neither in the United States nor in Barbados does one find too many groups effectively lobbying *against* tourism. Yet, there are those who have tried to arouse public concern for what they identify as negative effects of mass tourism. In the Caribbean, as in many other developing regions of the world, nationalist groups have spoken out against mass tourism; they have labelled it a new form of colonialism and imperialism. In the United States most opposition to tourism has been of an economic nature and there are patriotic overtones: Americans should "see the USA" first and should travel on U.S. carriers when they do go overseas.

This book, therefore, represents primarily an inquiry into national politics of two systems, centering upon those dimensions of political behavior which are evoked by a concern for international tourism. The framework is essentially one of domestic politics, but it does include the reality that often foreign actors are very much a part of national politics.

Tourism in the International Context

In 1974, international tourism was a $29 billion industry, measured in terms of foreign currency earnings by various countries. At the global level Western Europe accounts for over $20 billion of these earnings, or about 71%. And as Table 1 indicates, members of the Organization for Economic Cooperation and Development (OECD) together achieved 90% of the total world's earnings from international tourism in 1974.[1] On a world-wide basis developing countries have not yet achieved either by region or by nation a significant portion of world tourism revenues.

When one considers international tourism as distinct from domestic tourism, it is immediately understandable that Western Europe accounts for the bulk of the industry, in terms of receipts as well as in terms of arrivals (see Table 2). In comparison to other affluent regions such as Canada, the United States, and Japan, the countries of Western Europe are small in size and in close proximity to each other. In 1973 there were about 215 million international tourist arrivals throughout the world, of which 157 million or nearly 73% were in European countries. The Americas had 44 million arrivals, about 20% of the total. In the United States, as in Western European countries, the vast majority of visitors come from contiguous states. Of approximately 14 million visitors to the United States in 1973, only 3.5 million came from countries other than Canada and Mexico.[2]

TABLE 1

Foreign Currency Earnings from International Tourism of Various Countries and Regions, 1973 and 1974

Area	Amount (billions $ US) 1973	1974
Europe (OECD Members)	20.0	20.3
United States	3.2	4.0
Canada	1.4	1.5
Japan	.2	.2
Australia	.2	.2
Total World Earnings	28.0	28.8
OECD Members' Total	25.0 (89%)	26.4 (90%)

Source: OECD, *Tourism Policy and International Tourism in OECD Member Countries.*

TABLE 2

Tourists Arrivals by Region, 1973 and 1974

Region	Arrivals (millions) 1973	1974	% change
Europe	157.0	149.0	−5.1
Americas	44.0	46.0	+3.1
Pacific, East Asia	5.6	5.8	+4.5
Middle East	3.8	4.0	+5.3
Africa	2.9	3.0	+3.4
South Asia	1.1	1.1	+4.5
World Total	214.4	209.0	−3.0
OECD Countries	155.0 (72%)	145.0 (70%)	−7.0

Source: OECD, *Tourism Policy and International Tourism in OECD Member Countries.*

In addition to Western Europe and North America, Japan must be included as a metropolitan tourism marketplace. In 1973 over 2 million Japanese traveled abroad, mainly to the United States and Europe.[3] The potential of the Japanese market has been recognized by many governments which are now spending increasing amounts of money on advertising and promotion in that country.

In some countries international tourism has a truly prominent place in the overall economy. In Spain as much as 33% of all exports is represented by tourism earnings (see Table 3). In other states — Austria, Greece, Portugal, and Switzerland — tourism earnings represent a significant percent of total exports. In contrast, some large non-European states — the U. S., Canada, Australia, Japan and New Zealand — have a healthy tourism sector, but do not show more than 5% of total exports as tourism earnings. The situation of countries in this latter group is perhaps as reflective of their high export volume as it is of their absolute volume of tourism.

The pervading tourist flow continues to be between North America and Western Europe, mostly by air transport. Table 4 indicates that over 6.9 million passengers were flown across the North Atlantic to Europe in 1973 while over 5.7 million went in the other direction. Given the total of all air passengers in the world, both domestic and international (480 million in 1973), this European-North American traffic is substantial.[4] It is, in other words, the real artery of international tourism.

While Europe has always been the most popular destination of American travelers, only since 1970 or 1971 has its attraction in-

TABLE 3

Selected OECD Countries: Tourism Earnings as % of Exports and Tourism Expenditures as % of Imports, 1972

	Earnings/Exports	Expenditure/Imports
OECD European Countries	6.3%	5.4%
Austria	26.1	8.3
Spain	33.1	3.4
Greece	21.0	3.4
Portugal	18.1	5.7
Switzerland	11.7	6.1
Australia	2.0	5.0
Canada	4.9	5.7
Japan	.6	2.8
New Zealand	3.1	6.3
United States	3.7	6.2
TOTAL OECD COUNTRIES	5.2	5.4

Source: OECD, *Tourism Policy and International Tourism in OECD Member Countries*, p. 77.

TABLE 4

North Atlantic Air Passenger Traffic, 1973

	North America to Europe	Europe to North America	Total
Scheduled flights*	4,904,735	5,124.289	10,029,024
Charter	834,242	834,044	1,671,286
Total	5,738,977	6,961,333	11,700,310

* Members of International Air Transport Association.

Source: OECD, *Tourism Policy and International Tourism in OECD Member Countries*, pp. 53 and 82.

creased considerably in comparison to the Caribbean region. By 1973, over 3.8 million Americans embarked for European destinations while in the same year over 1.8 million went to the West Indies.[5] Both destination areas continue to have slight annual increases in the numbers of American visitors.

Tourism and International Relations

If 215 million visitors arrive in foreign countries in a given year, surely such an influx must affect relations among the world's various societies. The effects of tourism and tourists upon a given national group vary with the level and kind of tourism developed by that nation. In large and wealthy states (such as the United States and Canada), several million visitors per year may be accommodated without much disruption to the average citizen's life. In smaller countries and in poorer societies the tourism sector is highly visible and not only causes a disruption in the average citizen's life, but creates additionally a vision of affluence in stark contrast to surrounding poverty. In Barbados, which is by no means a poor country by world-wide development standards, tourism is an enormous industry which served in excess of 230,000 visitors in 1974.[6] The island's resident population of just over 250,000 lives on 166 square miles of land.

Tourism brings about a variety of changes in host societies. Some symptoms are obvious. As Howe Martyn has put it:

> A large influx of tourists has both a physical and a social impact. Tourists create objectionable conditions. They trample the grass. They track mud into the cathedrals, and make noise during services. However careful, they leave noticeable litter. They crowd buses and cafés, blocking out the natives. Furthermore, tourists appear to the local residents to pre-empt the best of everything — hotel rooms, food and rare wines, luxury products of all kinds, even the best looking girls.[7]

The ability of host residents to cope with these kinds of feelings and perceptions and the way they sort out valid objections from the spurious ones determine the image which the tourist leaves behind. The essential point is that international tourism leaves its mark more distinctly on those societies where the volume of tourism is high in comparison to the size of the population; or where the overall economic level of the host country is extremely below that of the tourist sector; or both! Where such conditions prevail, immediate changes occur in the behavior pattern of local people. As Davydd Greenwood reported in his study of a Spanish Basque community, "the rhythm of life in Fuenterrabia was totally altered."[8] Traditional occupations were disrupted, and the transition to a tourism economy meant among other things a nearly-total dependence upon external events.

In spite of negative effects of international tourism upon people, there are balancing arguments. The industry breeds a measure of international understanding and familiarity among peoples who otherwise might not be exposed to cultures other than their own. International travel promotes the brotherhood of mankind and uplifts, some say, the spirit. Government planners and economists suggest tourism growth as a desirable means of earning badly needed foreign exchange and of bolstering local productivity. Elites in some developing nations take pride in a modern tourism establishment and see hotels and airports as trappings of modernization. In other words, "it's nice to have lunch and a drink at the Hilton" or to know that several major airlines serve the country. And in some places such institutions of modernization come as a result of a growing or promising tourism business.

Besides the international relations of tourism brought about by a visitor-to-host relationship, there is also the interaction of groups, national and transnational, involved in the tourist industry. It is the dimension of world tourism which is most crucial to the continuation of the industry. We give here some of the international relationships which can be identified as tourism-centered.

First, international tourism hinges to a large extent upon a set of government-to-government relations. Agreements on air transport and airline routes are governmental matters. Although interested carriers are usually involved in negotiations for routes or route exchanges, it is primarily the responsibility and authority of their respective governments to work out such exchanges. In addition to air transport agreements governments must deal with other governments on a variety of problems vital to tourism: double taxation treaties, immigration and customs procedures, currencies and exchange rates, and general diplomacy for the protection of nationals traveling abroad.

A second set of international relationships vital to tourism is found in the interaction of national governments with foreign private enterprise. The establishment of a major hotel to be owned or operated by a foreign firm is preceded by months of negotiations between that firm and the host government. Officials dealing with subsidiaries of multinational corporations, for example, find that local managers can make only certain kinds of decisions while more important decisions must come from New York or London or wherever company headquarters are located. Corporate managers, as we shall see in Chapter 3, have similar difficulties in getting responses from host governments, especially in developing states.

These relations between governments and business take place in both the home territory of the government and in the corporation's country. Firms in search of investment opportunities tend to approach foreign governments on foreign soil, while government officials in search of new investment capital or technology for tourism will pay visits to the metropolitan centers of the world. Subsequent conferences and negotiations usually take place in the host country and usually involve various agencies or departments of government. Foreign airlines, for example, can approach the U.S. Civil Aeronautics Board or committees of the U.S. Congress as well as the Department of State.

A third cluster of international relations brought on by tourism and other multinational business is the continuous contact between parent corporations and their subsidiaries around the world. Hotel corporations, airlines, and banks maintain almost daily communication with their personnel in different countries. In some ways this contact can be seen as occurring within a national group, the corporation. But in reality there is an increasingly international composition to large tourism firms; through this communication process the conditions in respective countries are observed, analyzed, and acted upon. The importance of this kind of surveillance is confirmed by the long established practice of governments gaining intelligence information abroad through use of private business sources.

Finally, there is at least a fourth set of international relations identified with the growth of international tourism. International organizations are increasingly being used by governments, especially in developing nations, for planning and development of tourism. Regional groups such as the Organization of American States have undertaken ambitious programs for research, training, planning and development of integrated tourism sectors in member countries. The World Bank, while it has not allocated a significant portion of its capital to tourism, has forwarded funds to regional development banks like the Caribbean Development Bank which in turn support tourism projects. The United Nations, especially in its Conference on Trade and Development (UNCTAD), has recently increased its attention to tourism as a significant force in economic development.[9]

Other world-wide groups perhaps have a more direct influence upon tourism. The International Air Transport Association (IATA) is a non-governmental airline group which regulates voluntarily and through unanimous agreement of its members such things as international fares and inter-airline ticketing. The governmental counterpart of IATA is the International Civil Aviation Organization (ICAO) which operates as a specialized agency of the United Nations. Member governments (128) deal with more general matters of civil aviation than do IATA members, but both organizations are concerned with the promotion of cooperative and fair international air service. In some ways IATA has a more direct influence upon tourism because of its ability to set fares for international flights.

On November 1, 1974, the World Tourism Organization (WTO) was established as the newest intergovernmental tourism agency on a global level.[10] The WTO is partly, in its purposes, a continuation of two predecessor organizations: the International Union of Official Travel Organizations (IUOTO), organized in London in 1946; and the International Union of Official Tourist Publicity Organizations (IUOTPO) which was formed at The Hague in 1925. While the IUOTO was primarily a coordinating association for the collection and exchange of tourism information among member states, the new WTO has as its fundamental aim "the promotion and development of tourism with a view to contributing to economic development, international understanding, peace, prosperity, and universal respect for and observance of human rights and fundamental freedoms for all without distinction as to race, sex, language, or religion."[11] In working toward this goal the WTO intends to pay particular attention to needs of developing countries, and to collaborate with the United Nations and its appropriate specialized agencies.

Regional organizations are also spawned by tourism. In the Caribbean, since 1951, various governments and private institutions have coordinated tourism efforts through the Caribbean Tourism Association. The principal interest of this group is "support for development of the states of the Caribbean through tourism." Its membership includes regional governments, carriers which serve the Caribbean, and associate members such as hotel corporations. There are periodic conferences dealing with current tourism problems; and by 1975 the CTA had undertaken impressive and cohesive promotional efforts in the metropolitan markets, especially in the eastern U.S., stressing the attractiveness of the Caribbean region as a tourist destination. (For smaller countries such a regional approach to tourism promotion can be more efficient than for each state to rely solely on its own tourist boards.)

Like the World Tourism Organization, the CTA has more interests than just the promotion of tourism in member states. It is also concerned about the effects of the industry upon host populations and upon overall economic development. The new Caribbean Tourism Research Center in Barbados is a brain child of the CTA. The center has stated its intention to study all aspects of tourism as it affects Caribbean nations.

From the above discussion it is apparent that international tourism generates several kinds of transnational relations. Mass tourism further gives birth to many institutions which participate in these interstate affairs. It is mass tourism which has at the same time been subject to widespread criticism.

What is mass tourism and what are some of the criticisms of it which should be mentioned as we examine international contexts? The first images which come to mind are groups of people herded from place to place by tour guides (who presumably know something about the surroundings) — the "If it's Tuesday This Must Be Belgium" kind of approach. But mass tourism is really more than groups, tours, charters, or package holidays. It has come to mean all those tourists who patronize and depend upon the standard institutions of international tourism — the airlines, cruiseships, hotels, and various services intended primarily for tourists. Mass tourism has also come to connote foreign visitors who are arriving primarily for purposes of pleasure. OECD countries, however, define a tourist as "any person visiting a country, other than that in which he usually resides, for a period of at least 24 hours."[12] Thus, included are business travelers, persons attending conferences and persons visiting for pleasure. Also included are cruise passengers even if they stay less than 24 hours.

From the standpoint of immigration procedures such a definition as that of the OECD is a reasonable one. It does not, however, clarify our crude images of the mass tourist who usually has no business or professional reason for visiting a particular country and who, consequently, has placed himself at the mercy of the tourism institutions.

Erik Cohen has suggested a typology of international tourists which follows closely this image of the mass tourist.[13] He has described the following types: (1) the *organized mass tourist,* defined as in the image given above; (2) the *individual mass tourist,* who is not bound to a group but who nevertheless is dependent upon categorical planning; (3) the *explorer,* who arranges his own trip and who tries to get closer to the host culture while at the same time staying in comfortable quarters; and (4) the *drifter,* one who gets farther away from the tourism institutions and who tries to immerse himself in the host culture. Cohen sees the first two kinds of tourist roles as *institutionalized* and the last two as *non-institutionalized;* meaning simply that in the last two instances, tourism establishments play a less important role in the tourists' experience.

The mass tourist is one who is highly reliant upon tourism organizations for the planning and implementation of his visit. It is therefore the behavior of the mass tourist and his ancillary institutions which makes the politics of tourism an issue worth studying. The profits being made from mass tourism by an increasing number of companies and governments underlie the politics in question.

Some World-View Critiques of Tourism

Louis Turner has written that today's mass tourists are "the barbarians of our Age of Leisure."[14] They are "the visible expression of the fourth of the great technologically inspired waves which have since 1800 changed the social geography of the world."[15] Turner refers to jet travel which has been preceded by the railroads, the steamships, and the automobile. The jet age has made remote regions of the world accessible and attractive to hordes of metropolitan workers whose leisure and income have both been increasing. Like the barbarians of old, says Turner, the new masses come to stare gawkily at cultures remote from their own. They are vulgar, demanding, and often intolerant. They destroy a lot and learn very little. The mass extension of industrial culture through tourism represents a serious threat to the stability and sanity of the non-industrial peoples of the world. Such concerns are not shared by the tourism corporations whose chief motive is a return on investment.

As Turner sees it, these new Golden Hordes fan out to the exotic destinations of the world, to the sunbelt, the *pleasure periphery,* the equatorial zones of the earth, in search of the four s's of tourism — sun, sea, sand, and sex. From the Mediterranean to the Indian Ocean, from the Pacific to the Caribbean, this sun belt contains the traditional playgrounds of those whom Erik Cohen has called the *Nomads from Affluence.* While the legendary Golden Horde of Genghis Kahn's successors threatened the settled areas of Europe, this new golden horde of mass tourists threaten the less developed countries today. Their demands and the benefits offered to host people for meeting those demands bring moral, social and economic confusion to the playground cultures.

This critique of international mass tourism is primarily a social one, putting modern tourism into the world's social historical context. "Tourism as whorism" has become a popular phrase in many circles. The analogy is clear.

Others criticize tourism in more economic terms. It is often seen as a resurgence of colonialism and imperialism. Although legal relationships characteristic of colonialism have disappeared in most regions, the political and economic remnants remain. Metropolitan countries through imperialistic policies of business and investment still control most of the world's wealth and continue to have inordinate amounts of power over the lives of people in developing countries. Institutional tourism perpetuates this kind of relationship. Profits which accrue in the host counrty are not re-invested there, but rather are withdrawn to the parent company and to the metropolitan state. This critique portrays tourism more as *rape* than as *whorism.*[16]

Against the background of these perceptions, we now begin our examination of the politics of international mass tourism. These highly critical views of tourism as neo-colonialism or as the newest wave of barbarians are offset by nothing less than the *status quo;* tourism's critics are so far a small minority. Tourism growth seems to be the order of the day as long as the geese are willing to be herded onto aircraft and deposited in foreign playgrounds. The politics of such a vast activity then becomes a matter of who competes successfully for the privilege of being involved directly in *institutionalized* tourism.

NOTES
Chapter 1

[1] OECD members are: Australia, Austria, Belgium, Canada, Denmark, Finland, France, the Federal Republic of Germany, Greece, Iceland, Ireland, Italy, Japan, Luxembourg, the Netherlands, New Zealand, Norway, Portugal, Spain, Sweden, Switzerland, Turkey, the United Kingdom, and the United States.

[2] United States Travel Service, *1973: Tourism Action Year,* p. 29.

[3] OECD, *Tourism Policy and International Tourism in OECD Member Countries* (Paris: OECD, 1974), p. 45.

[4] *Ibid.* On all the scheduled airlines of the 128 member countries of ICAO.

[5] U. S. Travel Service, *Summary and Analysis of International Travel to the U. S.* (December 1974), p. 43.

[6] Central Bank of Barbados, *Economic and Financial Statistics* (June 1975), p. 48.

[7] Howe Martyn, "International Tourism," *Dalhousie Review,* vol. 50 (Spring 1970), p. 45.

[8] Davydd J. Greenwood, "Tourism as an Agent of Change: A Spanish Basque Case", *Ethnology,* vol. 2 (January 1972), pp. 80-91.

[9] See UNCTAD, *Elements of Tourism Policy in Developing Countries,* (New York: United Nations Publications, 1973), TD/B/C.3/89/Rev. 1.

[10] For a good summary of the creation of WTO and its predecessor organizations, see the entire issue of *Annals of Tourism Research,* vol. 2, no. 5 (May/June 1975).

[11] *Ibid.,* p. 251.

[12] OECD, *op. cit.,* p. 7.

[13] Erik Cohen, "Toward a Sociology of International Tourism", *Social Research,* vol. 39 (Spring 1972), pp. 164-182. See also his "Nomads from Affluence: Notes on the Phenomenon of Drifter-Tourism", *International Journal of Comparative Sociology,* vol. 14, nos. 1-2 (March-June 1973), pp. 89-103.

[14] Louis Turner and John Ash, *The Golden Horde* (London: Constables, 1975), p. 11.

[15] *Ibid.*

[16] See for example, Robert Wenkam, *The Great Pacific Rip Off: Corporate Rape in the Far East* (Chicago: Follett Publishing Co., 1974).

2
TOURISM POLITICS IN THE MARKETPLACE

The politics of world tourism are most intense in the metropolitan marketplace; it is there that one finds the greatest commercial efforts to transform the raw material — the tourists — into geese. But the success of the commercial effort is highly dependent upon a mastery of political technology by those actors who stand to gain from the flight of the geese to their resorts. In this application of political skill, tourism actors must seek favors from various administrative agencies of metropolitan governments as well as from legislative bodies. Airline routes, taxation policy, immigration restrictions, customs and currency — all are of vital importance to any tourism interest group with the profit motive in mind.

The potential rewards from these political efforts are seen in statistics. In 1973, the most recent good year for tourism, nearly 25 million U. S. residents visited foreign countries and spent $7 billion; the Canadians spent $1.7 billion abroad in the same year; and the Japanese spent about $1.3 billion. European members of OECD altogether spent $18 billion on foreign travel in 1973.[1] Tourists from these three regions (North America, Western Europe and Japan) accounted for at least $28 billion of the $29 billion in world tourism receipts in that year. This should be expected in light of the general income and leisure levels which have been attained in the metropolitan countries. There is little wonder, therefore, that the greatest commercial and political technologies in pursuit of tourism are to be found in these economies. It is there that the affluent geese reside.

The directional flow of tourists from the United States tells a great deal about the nature of international tourism. Canada attracts more American tourists than any other country, but more Americans go to Europe than to Mexico; this is despite the fact that Mexico is also a contiguous country and is relatively accessible. As Table 5 shows, the Caribbean is surely the North American Mediterranean with nearly 2 million visitors from the United States in 1973.

The contest for the buying of metropolitan tourists is, however, a two-way affair. While the private sector actors vie for increased sales, metropolitan nations struggle to maintain a balance of trade

TABLE 5

Directional Flow of American Travelers, 1973

Destination	Number of Travelers	% of total*
Canada	14,292,338	57.7
Europe	3,802,662	15.3
Mexico	2,829,890	11.4
West Indies	1,842,321	7.4
Asia	599,134	2.4
South America	314,286	1.2
Central America	180,772	.7
Oceania	116,466	.5
Africa	34,770	.1
Other overseas & cruise	741,676	3.0
Total	24,754,315	99.7

Source: U. S. Travel Service, *Summary and Analysis of International Travel to the U. S.* (December 1974), p .43.

* Column total does not equal 100 due to rounding.

with respect to travel and tourism. In the United States a persistent travel dollar deficit has been lessened in part by the economic recession which began around 1973 or a bit earlier (see Table 6). The Department of Commerce estimated that in 1974 this deficit would be less than $3 billion for the first time since 1971 (including fares).

In the large population centers, therefore, the politics of international tourism assumes two basic dimensions. First there is the struggle of the actors in the private sector who try to persuade these governments to allow them to sell foreign tourism to metropolitan consumers; second, there is the struggle of these same governments to protect their own interests by seeking a favorable balance in travel accounts. It is within these two dimensions of tourism politics that the intense competition for the tourist market can best be described.

The Important Private Actors

There are many competitors in tourism politics in the United States. Some are obviously of greater importance to the international industry than are others. In mass tourism the major political interest groups can be identified by following a sequence *typical* of the activities required in planning and purchasing an overseas holiday. First a typical consumer will contact a travel agent either for information or for purchasing service or both. Second, the typical international traveler uses air transport provided either by charter groups or by scheduled airlines. Third, this typical tourist is dependent upon hotels for accommodation wherever he goes. In

TABLE 6

Receipts, Expenditures and Travel Balances of Various Metropolitan Countries or Regions, 1973*

	Receipts	Expenditures	Balance
United States	3.2 billion	5.4 billion	—2.2 billion
Canada	1.4	1.7	— .3
European OECD	20.0	18.0	+2.0
Japan	.2	1.3	—1.1

Source: OECD, *Tourism Policy and International Tourism in OECD Member Countries*, pp. 51-52.

* Does not include fare payments.

addition, he depends upon financial institutions to provide essential services. This last group, made up mostly of banks and credit card companies, perhaps represent a fourth major tourism interest group in the marketplace. There are foreign counterparts to the four groups mentioned so far, which in a sense collectively amount to a fifth source of political pressure upon metropolitan national governments. In the United States foreign interests do lobby at various stages of policy-making. They are aided in this task by their own national governments which are rapidly discovering the importance of tourism to their countries. (Unlike goods or services, the flow of tourists into a country amounts to an export for that economy.)

The Travel Agents

In the metropolitan marketplace the tourists-geese first form lines at their respective travel agencies in search of details about possible destinations and the costs and means of getting there. As in real estate sales, the travel agent provides no absolutely essential service. Rather, he will sell a variety of required services to the customer for a fee which is paid by the seller. In comparison to airlines, travel agents do not appear as highly visible or as powerful in the articulation of their interests. Nevertheless, they are organized and have specified some of their political concerns.

The most important trade association for travel agents in the United States is the American Society of Travel Agents (ASTA), which has its headquarters in New York City and maintains legal counsel in Washington. ASTA represents about 5,000 travel agencies in the United States and Canada as well as over 1,000 tour operators and agents in 110 other countries. Its *active* members are year-round travel agents and operators while its *allied* members are airlines, steamship lines, rental car firms, hotels, bus lines, and others engaged in the travel business.

ASTA's stated purposes are twofold: (1) the promotion of the interests of the travel agency industry, and (2) the safeguarding of the traveling public against fraud, misrepresentation and other unethical practices.[2] Like many trade associations ASTA tries to serve as an ombudsman whenever a conflict arises in the triangular relationship involving government(s), the consumer, and the industry. ASTA also funnels information about changes in government policy to its member agencies, even though some notifications of policy changes, of course, go directly to the agencies from the Department of Commerce or from other appropriate agencies. ASTA attempts to keep its members informed of the ramifications of governmental policies by sponsoring periodic conferences and training sessions.

In its relationship with the U.S. Government, ASTA as lobbyist has been concerned with three important issues in recent years. First, the energy crisis has coincided with a period of inflation and recession, thereby multiplying its effects upon international travel. Government efforts to deal with that complex situation have been of concern to ASTA.

Second, the raging controversy over the Civil Aeronautics Board and its regulation of the airlines has been closely watched from the perspective of the travel agent. ASTA is not officially opposed to lower fares either on domestic or international flights; it is opposed to arrangements whereby tourists could by-pass the agent. There is no concerted effort to coordinate the views of the agents and the airlines on such matters, but in general ASTA is interested in any government policy which will eventually result in *dependable* commissions for agents. (In domestic politics this issue is almost entirely confined to the question of approval of fares which are cheaper because the passenger must purchase them from the airlines directly or at some designated location such as at an airport upon departure.) The CAB does not regulate the commission rate paid to agents by the airlines, but on international fares this rate has been established by IATA at 7½%. In the spring of 1975 an inter-airline dispute arose when Pan American World Airways, which had been suffering severe losses for some time, announced that it would pay travel agents a rate of 10% on sales in excess of 90% of the previous year for Pan Am. This action caused a furor in some circles. (The British Government on behalf of British Airways threatened to withdraw Pan Am's permit to operate in England and even to impound aircraft on the ground. This threat was averted by a British court which ruled in May, 1975,* that the British Government had no power to prevent Pan Am from paying the higher commission rate.)

---

* Subsequently, IATA was unable to reach agreement on commission rates for some months partly because that organization makes decisions on fare questions only through a 100% agreement of its membership; and although agents are not reluctant to accept the incentive commission from Pan Am, they and most governments want IATA to settle on a fixed commission

Agents make only about 7% commission on sales of airline tickets, but can make considerably more on group fares and on package sales. Thus, there has been agent support for relaxation of federal regulations on inclusive tour charters, a question which was resolved in 1975 when the CAB approved one-stop charters. Prior to that ruling, inclusive tour charters were required to stop at no fewer than three destinations at least 50 miles apart. The removal of this restriction is seen by most tourism actors as a boost for mass travel to sunspot desinations in the Caribbean, Mexico and Florida.

Finally, a third area of concern for travel agents as a political interest group has been the various federal changes in taxation policy affecting travel. ASTA has opposed measures which would discourage group foreign travel. Proposed changes in the Internal Revenue Code which would allow fewer deductions for international business travel, especially conventions, would fall into this category, as would most increased levies on airline tickets.

On a day-to-day basis, most lobbying by travel agent representatives is directed at regulatory agencies, the CAB in particular. The reasons for this are quite simple. The regulation of air transport, including the fare structures, most directly affects the income earning ability of agents. And lobbying the CAB requires an expertise not found among the agents themselves or among the traveling public. On the other hand, agents may be encouraged to contact members of Congress directly by mail, telephone or telegram on matters before that body since presumably congressmen and senators pay more attention to public opinion than do members of regulatory agencies.

On some issues the travel agent industry does not hold only one view. ASTA spokesmen claim that, for example, many agents encourage their customers to fly on U.S. carriers whenever possible, but some do not. Some want federal legislation requiring U.S. residents to patronize their country's flagships when departing and arriving in the United States. It seems unlikely that any single view of that question will become a basis of interest articulation for the travel agents. As we shall see in a subsequent section, however, the welfare of U.S. carriers *vis-a-vis* foreign airlines has become a mild political issue.

Travel agents, who generally earn their living entirely by commissions, generally favor decisions which will increase commissions — either through higher fares or through higher volume as a

---

rate. In reality the issue could become more complex in that other international airlines might increase their rates and rationalize the increase on the grounds of badly needed foreign exchange. To many U. S. carriers this practice amounts to a price war, something which they have usually opposed.

result of increased accessibility to the market. In this overall pursuit, what are some specific issues, and how have the agents and their lobbyists exercised political action?

Representatives of ASTA often appear as witnesses before Congressional committees on matters of importance to the travel industry. In March, 1975, for example, James Miller, an ASTA Vice President, appeared before the Subcommittee on Transportation and Commerce of the House Committee on Interstate and Foreign Commerce. He offered support for Congressional appropriation to the U.S. Travel Service for promotion of tourism to the United States. Miller appeared as a member of a panel of witnesses from the Discover America Travel Organization, Inc., an association of over 600 tourism groups whose main goal is the promotion of tourism in the United States. ASTA has also lobbied in favor of more competitive charter flight arrangements. It supported the One-Stop Tour Charter (OTC) which was approved by the CAB in 1975.

The Airlines

In the politics of mass tourism today, there is no more aggressive and complicated lobby than the airlines. Modern air transport on both scheduled and supplemental carriers is the key to world travel, and likewise is the most involved political interest group of all those concerned with international tourism. There are several reasons why this is the case. For example, there are those governments which see their own international airlines as a source of prestige and as a means of earning foreign exchange. International air transport, for industrial nations, is the precursor of expanding trade. It is also a visible mode of diplomatic contact.

In developing nations the governmental desire to have one's own international carrier seems to be based more on nationalism than on sound economic reasoning. By operating a national airline into foreign countries, a government not only earns badly needed foreign exchange but it also retains currency from its own citizens who travel and who otherwise would become a source for foreign exchange for foreign governments. The economic importance of airlines is diminished for most non-industrial states because of the necessity to purchase, maintain and operate the aircraft using foreign expertise and capital. Thus, the overwhelming factor in the desire for a national carrier in many developing countries must be prestige and nationalism. In some economies an airline presents an *image* of modernization and technical achievement.

This prestige is exploited by developing governments both at home and abroad. It is a ploy to foster domestic political support and at the same time to convey to the outside world an image of modernity. Even if some international airlines are malconceived, economically speaking, once they exist there is a tendency to treat them as sacred cows. Governments, the business community, and ordinary citizens come to believe that the nation's future somehow is coincidental with the continued operation (even at a loss) of the nation's carrier. This fixation is particularly true of small developing nations which often have only one carrier.

There is general agreement that the economic return of airlines is small in terms of a total national economy except in certain atypical situations.[3] In the case of extremely small countries, for instance, where there is heavy incoming international travel, an airline might well be worthy of a national effort. And if an airline is successful in becoming a regional carrier, the gamble would pay off. In small developing states the employment generated by an airline remains small in terms of numbers of jobs, and many airlines which have achieved regional recognition continue to operate at a loss. This loss is most often absorbed by the carrier's national government in order to "keep the flag flying." Nationalism becomes the prevailing motivation.

Regardless of how and why airlines are established, the fact is that they are today the most crucial factor in world travel and tourism. Whereas once practically all of the world's carriers, whether airline or steamship, were metropolitan in ownership, today's travelers can choose from well over 100 scheduled air carriers representing many countries. The existence of a strong tourism potential has stimulated many nations to enter the airline business. Small countries in the Caribbean — Barbados, Jamaica, Trinidad-Tobago — have national carriers operating to the metropoles of North America and Europe. Of the three, Air Jamaica has achieved the highest reputation as an efficiently-run airline, perhaps because it began under the close supervision of Air Canada. Now it operates entirely with Jamaican personnel.

Air routes. — The input of airlines to the politics of international tourism begins with the establishment of international routes. Tourism often is the primary justification for some of these routes. For the United States Government, for example, the legal prerogative for establishing bilateral agreements and reciprocal air service with other countries is in the statutory charge of the Civil Aeronautics Board. The promotion and regulation of international air service is intended to encourage and develop "an air transportation system properly adapted to the present and future needs of the foreign and domestic commerce of the United States, of the postal service, and of national defense."[4] While other governments as well are motivated by similar concerns, the airlines themselves are moved by desires for profit; hence, they apply to fly those designated routes on which they feel that a return can be expected.

The establishment of international routes begins with negotiations between govermnents; these result in legal agreements detailing the terms of the exchange of air service. Each government in turn then issues operating permits to both its own designated carrier on the route and to the carrier designated by the foreign government. For the United States, a typical negotiating team would include representatives from the Department of State, the CAB, the Air Transport Association of America, and perhaps someone from the U.S. carrier designated for the route. On occasion the White House will be represented as well.

At this stage of tourism politics, the political interests of the airlines are closely intertwined with their legal interests. Officials of the Air Transport Association (ATA) and of the individual airlines combine their talents to see that negotiations concerning routes and reciprocal service conform to previously established agreements. Most important among these agreements are the Chicago Convention of 1944 and the Bermuda Agreements of 1946. Politically, these interest groups work through the CAB, IATA, and with foreign carriers and governments in an effort to protect the interests of U.S. airlines *vis-a-vis* foreign carriers. This includes concern for fares and fare structures, safety standards, flight frequencies, and so forth. U.S. carrier interests in such matters are articulated primarily by the ATA spokesmen; U.S. supplemental airlines look to the National Air Carrier Association (NACA) for the promotion of their interests on similar matters.

The United States Government tends to negotiate rather carefully on air route matters, at least in comparison with European countries. Once the CAB approves a new route it exercises little further control over the operation of the foreign carrier on matters such as flight frequencies. It has the authority to do so, but the U.S. interpretation of international law leads to support for open competition on a route once it is established.

There is a feeling among some CAB officials that many foreign carriers have managed to survive only because of the rather open operating arrangement into major U.S. cities. Each time the U.S. wants a new route to a foreign country it must at the same time be willing to allow entry to a foreign carrier on that same route. Just after World War II the United States was inclined to be generous with such routes because there were few carriers and because such routes facilitated the economic recovery of Europe and Japan. But today the U.S. is being forced to re-examine its international aviation policy with an eye toward curbing foreign access to the American market and toward improving the competitive position of U.S. carriers on those existing international routes. Many other countries are adopting similar caution. For the United States, however, the problem is brought on by the recent proliferation of small foreign carriers and by the fact that the U.S. is the most lucrative market.

As an example of this problem, and of this U.S. re-examination, let us consider an instance where the Peruvian government wanted additional routes into the United States; its weapon in the quest was to deny Braniff International Airways freedom to serve secondary cities in Peru and elsewhere in South America after once landing in Lima. Braniff argued, as did the CAB, that market demands in the U.S. were insufficient to warrant additional flights and that the trade-off was unfair. Partly because of this unwillingness by the CAB to grant additional South American routes, the Government of Peru issued orders in the Fall of 1974 for Braniff to reduce the number of weekly flights from the U.S. to Lima.*

This conflict over international air services between the U.S. and Peru was a situation in which both governments were attempting to protect their respective interests. The U.S. view was that since most traffic on these routes was generated in the U.S., it was only reasonable that Braniff operate more frequently than AeroPeru, or at least as frequently as the market demanded. Additionally, the U.S. protested the Peruvian curtailment of Braniff's operation because of the U.S. philosophy that once routes are established such matters as frequency of service are for open competition to determine. Latin Americans tend to interpret reciprocity and equality to mean equal numbers of flights by both countries.[5]

Many Latin Americans believed sincerely that the political clout of Braniff in the U.S. was what caused the CAB to deny additional routes, but CAB personnel saw a situation in which there were two differing interpretations of international agreements and procedure. In the CAB's view, the Peruvian interpretation would lead to unreasonable exploitation by a small foreign airline of the U.S. travel market. At least according to some critics, this difference in views of international air law will likely lead to other disputes between the U.S. and Latin American countries.

Regulation of Fares. — Once airlines have established themselves on international routes, politics then center upon such matters as fares, the kind of service including frequencies, and occasionally a route exchange between carriers of the same nationality. In a large and complex country such as the United States the domestic political efforts of airlines are much greater than the international activities. That is, the CAB and other governmental agencies are continually under greater scrutiny for the

---

* The CAB retaliated in the Spring of 1975 by reducing the operation of AeroPeru to one weekly round-trip between Lima and Miami. Peru reacted in kind by reducing Braniff's New York to Lima service to one trip per week. . . . After considerable government-to-government and carrier-to-carrier negotiation, near-normal traffic was restored. Out of the conflict, the Peruvians succeeded in getting new routes to Los Angeles and New York, while Braniff was able to recover some of its service beyond Lima. The CAB was accused of serving the interests of Braniff. The problem reflected the reality that metropolitan travelers in the United States are the prime market for both U. S. carriers and foreign ones.

domestic effects of their regulation than for the international aspect. Our focus here is upon the politics of *international* tourism, and therefore any review of domestic airline politics in the marketplace is undetailed except as it might affect international travel.

Although the United States Government through its CAB does not establish international fares, it must approve or disapprove of those set by IATA. But the CAB can also affect international fares through its regulation of certain domestic fares. A tourist enroute from Los Angeles to Barbados has his fare calculated by adding together the domestic portion and the international portion. Thus, the maintenance of a high domestic fare surely influences the consumer's choice of whether he will vacation in Barbados, in Miami, or just forget about flying and drive to Mexico!*

In the mid-1970's the whole issue of airline regulation promises to be an issue of deep ideological cleavage in the United States. Many political conservatives want less regulation of fares and flight frequencies because fewer restrictions are consistent with capitalistic/conservative thought. Some liberals agree with the conservative position but for different reasons: competition would lead to lower fares and scores of less wealthy people could then afford to fly. Even more importantly though, the liberals in Congress charge that the CAB would lose its role as protector of the airlines' interests and could become more a servant of the consumers' needs. Ralph Nader's Aviation Consumer Action Project put it this way before a Senate sub-committee: the CAB is "little more than a government sponsored trade association."[7]

The airline industry and proponents of continued regulation of the industry obviously disagree. They argue for "enlightened regulation" as opposed to reduced regulation.[8] Of most concern to the industry, however, is the idea of open or free entry into the business. As new carriers exercise the right to enter the airline business, others could exercise their right to free exit. As a consequence, the industry's spokesmen say, larger cities would naturally attract the best airline service while smaller communities would be less

---

* A case in point occurred in March 1975 when World Airways filed application with the CAB for permission to fly passengers from coast to coast in the U. S. for an $89 fare each way, about one third of the regular fare at the time of filing. If such an arrangement were to be approved, it could be a strong inducement for international travel which must begin with a transcontinental flight. Needless to say, the new fare was immediately opposed by the larger scheduled carriers on the grounds that it was not a realistic one in light of ever-higher operating costs for all airlines. In the view of TWA President Tillinghast, if such a fare were approved, other carriers would match it, all would have lower load factors than expected by World Airways, and eventually all but one carrier would go out of business.[6] From this point of view it could be argued that the results of open competition would be calamitous.

well provided for or would lose all scheduled air facilities. Fares on remaining routes, however, probably would drop in price at least initially. In other words, under complete de-regulation chaotic competition would result and the public interest would not be served. Some industrialists believe that talk of airline de-regulation is little more than a way for politicians to garner support for their next election. As it stands, the debate seems filled with ideological paradoxes. In 1976, for instance, President Ford's support for de-regulation did not coincide with views held by the traditionally conservative elements in the Republic Party, especially management.

This issue concerning how airlines should be regulated has one major implication for international tourism. If de-regulation is to be the order of the day, then what constitutes "public need and convenience" must be reconsidered. Is it in the national interest that American carriers fly to such popular tourist areas as Acapulco, Fiji, Barbados or St. Lucia? If so, is that interest sufficient to justify subsidizing carriers so that they break even or make a small profit? Once carriers are free to give up routes that are unprofitable, then someone, presumably government, must make those routes worthwhile if the airlines are to continue meeting the public needs beyond the tourist traffic.

With respect to international fares, however, de-regulation of the U.S. domestic air service would have little effect as fares of IATA members are regulated by that body, and only carriers which do not belong to that group can offer lower prices. IATA attempts to police its membership also on other practices such as illegal discounts, commissions to travel agents, and rebates.

Efforts by newcomers to the international air transport business to establish cheaper fares, particularly in the North Atlantic, have not been well received by all governments or by IATA. In the North Atlantic market the most controversial attempt to reduce fares was proposed by Laker Airways. Its owner, Freddie Laker, received a license as early as 1972 from the British Government to operate as a third British flag carrier to the United States. He was licensed to operate out of Stansted Airport, south of London; and on the American end he hoped to use Kennedy Airport in New York. The new service was to be a shuttle type operation called Skytrain, using DC-10 aircraft and flying passengers one way for $135, tickets to be bought at the terminal within six hours of departure.

In 1975 Laker was still attempting to get CAB approval in the United States. Earlier, in October 1974, Laker filed suit in British courts accusing four carriers — TWA, Pan Am, British Airways, and British Caledonian — of conspiring to prevent his Skytrain operation from being approved by the U.S. Civil Aeronautics Board. The same suit was filed in U.S. District Court in Washington. As one Laker attorney states, "We have a British license to take our chance with our own money, in the tourist marketplace. If we are deprived of that right, through the actions of a cartel, then we have a right to go to the law courts."[9]

In Laker's view the primary justification for his suit lay in the fact that Britain and the United States reached a new agreement on capacity over the North Atlantic in 1974, but a clause was inserted to the effect that the agreement itself would be void if another airline in addition to the four already operating entered the picture. Laker Airways would be that new carrier, and it had been already approved by the British Government! Although some consumer groups in the U. S. had favored the Laker operation and the new low trans-Atlantic fares, the CAB had not issued a permit. Laker accused the CAB and others of political conspiracy to keep his airline from entering the market.

The Laker affair continues to affect (unofficially) the development of tourism between the U.S. and the eastern Caribbean. For some years Laker has operated International Caribbean Airways — between London and Barbados *via* Luxembourg. The round-trip fare advertised in 1975 was £120, or just under $300. In late 1974 the Barbados Government succeeded in procuring 51% of the airline *ownership* and ICA now advertises as the *national* carrier of Barbados. It has sought permission to serve three eastern cities in the U.S., but approval has not been forthcoming from the CAB. This inaction of CAB reflects in part a concern for Laker's involvement with International Caribbean Airways. (There is the question whether the Barbados Government really owns the airline or whether the arrangement is merely a convenience). The CAB is obviously not anxious to approve a permit for an airline owned in whole or in part by a man who has accused that agency of political conspiracy against him.

Although the matter of International Caribbean Airways' operation to the U. S. from Barbados will likely be resolved, the question of substantially lower fares in the North Atlantic will always be an issue, mainly because of the volume of passenger traffic there and because of the carrier reliance upon that route for profits to cover other routes with losses.

In some ways the politics of international fares can be as complicated as that of domestic fares. IATA members cannot undercut fares established by that association, but such fares are at the same time the result of unanimous agreement. The efforts by major IATA carriers to keep fares at an acceptable level in terms of costs, safety and profits require political efforts at both the international and the domestic levels. Fares which have been set by IATA are also subject to approval by the individual carrier's government.

It is inherent in the concept of state sovereignty that national governments have the right to allow or disallow fares on flights which deposit or pick up traffic in their national territory. A nation's airlines can capitalize upon this right by relying upon their government to protect them whenever a cut-rate fare is proposed by a foreign carrier or indeed by one of the same nationality. In the Laker incident described above, the CAB was able to deny Laker permission to commence operation even though the British Government had granted license to operate. The CAB certainly considered the effects of a new service and a new low fare upon American, TWA, and Pan American Airways, which must compete with about 20 foreign carriers which fly the same east-west route.

TABLE 7

North Atlantic Scheduled Passengers and Load Factors, By Carrier, 1974

Carrier	Number of Passengers	Average Load Factor
Trans World	1,586,733	52.9%
Pan American	1,389,197	53.6
British Airways	1,057,046	62.3
Air Canada	682,651	66.9
Lufthansa	612,059	63.6
Air France	609,732	65.1
KLM	497,015	55.6
Alitalia	457,090	53.8
SAS	388,389	61.0
Swissair	372,037	58.2
Iberia	295,727	55.6
CP Air	260,988	64.4
El Al Israel	244,195	71.8
Sabena	219,034	62.2
Irish Int'l	213,438	65.0
Olympic	144,119	56.4
TAP	109,314	54.1
Air India [1]	72,923	48.5
British Caledonian [2]	66,012	45.8
LOT	32,393	72.4
Finnair	28,849	45.0
TOTAL	9,338,941	58.2
U.S. Flag Total	2,975,930	53.2
Non-U.S. Flag Total	6,363,011	60.9

[1] On strike approximately 4 months.

[2] Operations for first 10 months only.

Source: *Aviation Week and Space Technology* (April 21, 1975), pp. 38-39.

Of the 9,338,941 scheduled passengers who flew over the North Atlantic in 1974, 2,975,930 or about 32% were carried on the two U.S. airlines.

In 1973, almost 7,000,000 American residents departed for foreign destinations other than Canada or Mexico. Better than 50% of their expenditures on flying was earned by foreign airlines.[10] With respect to 1972, Blaine Cooke of Trans World Airlines put it rather bluntly:

> In 1972, 65 percent of international departures were Americans but only 55 percent flew American. The result was that although we earned $900 million from foreigners, they earned $1.4 billion from us, or we (the U. S.) lost around $500 million in the balance of payments exchange.[11] (parenthesis mine)

This imbalance in favor of foreign carriers has led to some generalized statements outside of government that "a rape of the American market place" is indeed occurring. In the early 1970's for example, a group called Citizens for "America Comes First" advocated legislation which would require that all U.S. citizens patronize national flag carriers when traveling between the U.S. and foreign points. Further, this group advocated an open door policy for foreign airlines into the U.S., including freedom to transport foreign nationals between major American cities.[12] Such actions in the view of this organization would improve the revenues and volume of U.S. international carriers and would stop the so-called rape of the American market by foreign carriers. At the same time it could increase foreign travel to the U.S. through lower fares which would result from increased volume. These rather radical recommendations, however, apparently were not tolerable to industry and government leaders.

A 1970 White House *Statement of International Air Transportation Policy* recommended among other things that: (1) in the exchange of air routes care must be taken to "assure U.S. air carriers the opportunity to achieve benefits no less than those available to the foreign air carriers," and (2) that the U.S. "should take appropriate measures against carriers of foreign countries restricting U.S. carrier operations in violation of the terms of bilateral agreements or of the principle of reciprocity."

Other aspects of international air service have been periodically reviewed by the U.S. Government. These included, as early as 1970, a concern for changes in charter regulation, the need for cheaper promotional fares in the Pacific region and experimental promotion fares in general within the machinery of IATA. Throughout most reviews of U.S. international aviation policy in recent years two themes have been stressed: (1) the maintenance of fair competition between U.S. and foreign airlines, and (2) the effects of the U.S. carrier positions upon the overall balance of payments problem. This latter concern could include approval of marketing techniques which might increase the inbound traffic to the United States. Similar aspects of international aviation policy came up again for study in the Ford Administration in early 1975.

Industry spokesmen have usually summarized the problem of unfair competition for U.S. international carriers in terms of differing political systems and ideologies. They have repeatedly pointed out that most foreign carriers are owned in whole or in part by their governments. They do not have the problem of balancing the books or turning a profit. Their losses are absorbed in one form or another by government appropriations. In the face of such foreign conditions and competition, U.S. carriers have sought increased subsidy on international routes for some time. Also, in the view of at least one industry executive, foreign carriers do not necessarily believe in competition among themselves.[13] Instead, they engage in pooling, a practice of sharing revenues on a given route regardless of which carrier accommodated the passenger. Faced with this kind of *competition,* two carriers, TWA and Pan Am, sought permission to swap certain international routes in 1975 as a solution to some of their persistent losses. In the same year, the CAB approved certain route exchanges between Pan Am and American Airlines in the Caribbean and in the Pacific.

Charters. — The United States Government enters into agreements with foreign countries for charter flights as separate from scheduled service. In Chapter 1 (Table 4) we saw that just over one tenth of all North Atlantic air passengers flew on chartered service in 1973; yet, still, one-tenth amounted to 1.6 million people. If one looks at the charter traffic from the U.S. marketplace (Table 8), the total volume is truly impressive. In 1974 over 3.8 million passengers to and from the U.S. used this type of service. United States carriers fly a greater portion of this traffic than they do of scheduled passengers. Over 72% of these 3.8 million people flew on U.S. carriers either supplemental or route, both of which are entitled to provide charter service under approved conditions. In other words, where charter service has been authorized by the CAB, the regular route carriers as well as supplemental airlines can offer the service to interested groups.

In the U.S., the most pressing issue concerning charters has been the desire for one-stop tour charters (OTC's). Prior to 1975 the CAB required that inclusive tour charters (ITC's) be at least seven days in duration, that they stop at three destination cities not less than 50 miles apart, and that the total package price be at least 110% of the lowest available air fare for that trip. For years these requirements had impeded the operation of inclusive tour charters to such places as the Caribbean. Many remote islands in that region could have substantially increased the number of American visitors if ITC's had been able to fly directly to one destination and return. The Canadians have been allowing one-stop tour charters for some time to points in the Caribbean. U.S. supplementals have argued that they could provide a package OTC for much less than 110% of the lowest air fare and that the price of such tours had been kept high by the CAB regulations.

TABLE 8

Numbers of Passengers Carried by U. S. International Charter Flights, by Region, 1974

Region	No. of Passengers	Totals
Transatlantic		2,365,518
U. S. Route Carriers	605,195	
U. S. Supplementals	1,099,916	
Foreign Route Carriers	326,205	
Foreign Charter Carriers	334,202	
Transpacific		363,415
U. S. Route Carriers	180,981	
U. S. Supplementals	112,949	
Foreign Route Carriers	69,485	
Foreign Charter Carriers	—	
Latin Am/Caribbean		806,225
U. S. Route Carriers	589,746	
U. S. Supplementals	159,144	
Foreign Route Carriers	55,430	
Foreign Charter Carriers	1,905	
Canada		352,890
U. S. Route Carriers	51,312	
U. S. Supplementals	22,210	
Foreign Route Carriers	24,856	
Foreign Charter Carriers	254,512	
Total U. S. Route Carriers		1,427,234
Total U. S. Supplemental Carriers		1,394,219
Total Foreign Route Carriers		475,976
Total Foreign Charter Carriers		590,619
Grand Total All Charters from U. S.		3,888,048

Source: National Air Carrier Association compiled from CAB Form 41 Reports, Schedule T-6 and CAB Form 217. Converted to Passengers using a factor of 90% for 1974.

In 1975 the CAB in the United States did revise its charter regulations. It approved the OTC with a minimum tour duration of four days in North American destinations and seven days elsewhere. It set no specific charter rates for the OTC except that it should be at least $15 per night of the tour in addition to the cost of the air transportation. The approval of this plan was lauded by the National Air Carrier Association, which represents supplemental carriers. It had long supported and worked for such change.

The scheduled carriers were not unified in their view of these new guidelines. United Airlines and Pan American World Airways did voice approval, but since no general agreement existed among the schedued carriers, the Air Transport Association did not lobby the CAB on the matter. Eastern Airlines, whose service from the U. S. to the Caribbean has grown substantially in recent years, objected to the OTC plan. They countered the new provisions by offering a new reduced-rate *individudal tour filing* on their U. S.-Florida-Caribbean routes.[14] Their officers felt that it was unable to release aircraft from scheduled service in order to compete for OTC customers.

The new CAB regulations also made it possible for passengers to take advantage of charter rates without belonging to an affinity group. Such requirements had come under increasing criticism as being unfair and continually abused. No lengthy advance purchase time is now required for such travel.

The airline lobbies. — In addition to each individual airline indulging in political efforts, there are in the U. S. two important trade associations which lobby the government on behalf of their members. The National Air Carrier Association (NACA) represents the four major supplemental airlines in the United States: World Airways, Trans International, Saturn, and Overseas National. The four carriers account for about 95% of the traffic on non-route carriers. These carriers specialize in charter operations to the Pacific region, Europe, the Caribbean, and Mexico. From their Washington offices NACA staff persons promote and protect the interests of the supplemental carriers before several governmental agencies. They monitor Congressional activities which might affect these interests, and they keep in close contact with the policy questions before the CAB.

Of course, in most instances the interests of supplemental airlines and the interests of scheduled carriers are in conflict. And for NACA, major lobbying efforts stem from closely watching the political efforts of the scheduled carrier representatives, especially as they affect changes in the relative competitive ability of the smaller charter lines.

NACA deals primarily with policy questions. It must maintain data to support the interest articulation of the supplemental carriers. But once a policy matter is settled, NACA's involvement ceases, and each individual member airline becomes responsible for translating the new policy into marketing arrangements or into operational terms.

Although NACA deals also with the domestic operations of its members, its importance to the politics of international tourism can be found in the various struggles over international aviation policy. In recent years the chief concerns have been the regulation of charter fares by the CAB and the drive for CAB approval of OTC's. With permission to operate charter tours to one destination for a four-day minimum stay, the supplementals see new market possibilities in the so-called, sun-spots of the Caribbean, Florida, Arizona, Southern California, Hawaii, and Mexico. Europe has been the major destination of U. S. supplemental carriers in the past. In 1974 of the 1,394,219 passengers flown by these carriers, over 1 million of them were transatlantic traffic.

U. S. scheduled carriers are important to international tourism in that they either transport passengers to foreign destinations or they feed into those which do, or both. Eastern Airlines, for example, has developed an extensive network of service from the eastern U. S. to various parts of the Caribbean using San Juan, Puerto Rico as a hub. In 1975 American Airlines replaced Pan American as the direct carrier between New York and Barbados in the eastern Caribbean. The domestic marketing ability of American Airlines made it an attractive carrier to the Barbados Government. Tourists could more easily fly from various cities in the U. S. through New York to Barbados on a single carrier.

In terms of lobbying, the scheduled U. S. carriers rely on at least three levels of political organization: a national association, an inter-airline Washington Committee, and each individual airline. The Air Transport Association of America (ATA), which has 24 members and 2 associate members, represents all major scheduled carriers. The ATA staff members who specialize in government relations or international operations continuously maintain a dialogue with the appropriate government offices. This includes monitoring of legislative activity in various committees, and holding conferences almost daily with personnel at the CAB, the Department of State, or the Department of Transportation. The ATA has a vice president for international affairs and a vice president for federal affairs. Together they work to assure through the political process (lobbying) as much protection for the interests of their members as possible. At the international level the efforts of ATA include keeping the State Department informed of any problems encountered by member carriers on international flights. Such matters as safety procedures, landing rights, harassment from foreign institutions, or violations of accepted international aviation procedures by a competitor would all fall into this category of activity. Additionally, the ATA provides data and special studies for use by member airlines in their publications or in their own dealings with federal, state and local government, as well as with foreign governments.

The second type of organization used by airlines in their relations with the U. S. government is an inter-airline Washington committee. This group functions both as an advisory body to ATA and as a group working to synthesize or formulate an industry view on policy questions. If there is not a unified view, then each airline undertakes its own lobbying for or against a particular issue. When a consensus view is obtained, then ATA can proceed to lobby along with each member airline at the appropriate levels of government.

At the third level, each airline maintains its own staff, usually in Washington, for dealing with governmental affairs. Smaller airlines will utilize established law firms or other professional lobbyists for this purpose. On important federal issues there will be close coordination between all three levels of airline organization.

Foreign carriers also lobby the U. S. Government, but since so many of them are government owned, they rely upon their own national executive for this kind of assistance. The filing of a formal application with the CAB for a new route is in itself a type of lobbying because it forces a question of policy upon decision-makers. For instance, British West Indian Airways, the national airline of Trinidad-Tobago, has asked the CAB for a route serving Houston, but little progress was made on the application for several years because the Government of Trinidad-Tobago had other priorities including talks with Soviet Officials concerning possible air links between the two countries. While BWIA managers are eager to obtain this new route into the US., they must depend on their national leaders to effect it.

In the metropolitan marketplace the airline lobby is probably the most important of all to the flow of international tourism. Although all of the world's carriers are in a sense competing for the transport of American geese, the U. S. airlines dominate the political scene in Washington. All carriers have been injured severely by increased fuel costs, inflation, recession, and the general decline in holiday travel abroad since about 1972 or 1973. They have had a great deal at stake in the political phase of world tourism. But as Table 9 indicates, U. S. carriers appear to have even more at stake in domestic air service. Although 1974 was a bad year for airlines in general, Table 9 shows that on international runs most carriers registered severe losses in that year. These same carriers immdiately set to work with other airlines to lessen the impact of these losses. It should be stressed, however, that whenever these changes involved foreign governments, the airlines negotiated with those states along with assistance from the United States Government.

TABLE 9

Net Profits of U. S. A. Air Carriers, Domestic & International Routes, 1974

Carrier	Profit or (loss) $ millions Domestic	International
American	12.9	—
American (LAD)	—	8.1
American (Pacific)	—	(.7)
Braniff	17.1	10.3
Continental	9.8	(1.7)
Delta	86.1	1.2
Eastern	28.1	(17.7)
National	19.8	1.5
Northwest	50.2	14.5
Trans World	(.3)	—
TWA (Atlantic)	—	(81.7)
TWA (Pacific)	—	(22.4)
TWA (non-div.)	—	(12.3)
United	92.2	—
Western	21.6	—
Pan American	—	(81.7)

Source: *Aviation Week and Space Technology* (June 2, 1975), p. 41.

Airlines lobby in yet another way. Like many other corporations, some airlines have sought political influence through financial losses. Their efforts have included requests for government subsidies, proposals to drop some routes and to exchange others, and contributions to congressional or presidential election campaigns. In May 1975 the CAB fined American Airlines $150,000 for using corporate funds as political contributions, including $55,000 allocated for President Nixon's re-election in 1972.[15] Also in 1975, the CAB's Bureau of Enforcement accused Braniff Airways of raising some $641,000 and possibly another $286,000 through issuance and sale of 3,626 unaccounted tickets. The airline contributed $40,000 of these monies to Nixon's campaign in 1972.[16]

It was an unusual election year which attracted the attention of the business world more than in most years. If the Watergate crisis had not developed as it did, Nixon would have been in a position to pass out favors to those companies which had supported him. The stakes for airlines were high. Given the economic slump in the U. S. and throughout the world, air carriers needed all the government help they could get, and Nixon had long before achieved a reputation of remembering his friends and enemies. Too, Senator George McGovern's stance on broad social and economic questions was basically opposed to the interests of big business. For these reasons many corporate leaders rallied to Nixon's re-election effort, and that some did so through completely illegitimate means indicates the apparent influence of the chief executive over airline regulation.

Other Tourism Lobbies

Although the airline industry perhaps overshadows all tourism lobbies in the United States (especially with respect to American travel abroad), several other interests must be mentioned in order to complete our typical journey. Airlines, for example, are dependent upon banks. Banks own aircraft and lease them to the airlines while both institutions benefit tax-wise in the process. Banks can facilitate tourism development abroad and at home by making available lines of credit to institutions such as hotels, airlines, and credit card companies.

Hotels and credit card companies, like other special-interest groups pursue their political needs both through membership in trade associations and through their own individual actions. The American Hotel and Motel Association (AHMA) regularly presents the hotel industry point of view to policymakers in Washington. However, large international hotels do not always find their interests coincidental with those of domestic industry. When that occurs, the larger U. S. hotel firms will rely upon their own personnel for lobbying efforts rather than upon the associations. A major American multinational firm, Hilton International Corporation, does not have an executive post devoted entirely to governmental affairs. Political issues are often dealt with by appropriate executives in the firm. If an issue is primarily a concern of marketing, then personnel in that office will in effect take on the role of lobbyist. In the case of Hilton International much of its political interest can be articulated by its owner, Trans-World-Airlines. In a general sense at least, what is good for TWA is good for Hilton International.

The tendency, therefore, is to utilize industry-wide associations for dealing with the U. S. Government on tourism issues whenever possible. Depending upon the relative size and affluence of particular interest groups, some will also maintain strong governmental relations of their own. Both approaches represent important sources of pressure upon policymakers.

The Metropolitan Government and International Tourism

Today, most national governments attempt to attract foreign tourists as a means of achieving export earnings. Few governments openly promote the foreign travel of their own citizens, although it could be argued that the more open a society claims to be, the fewer restrictions there are upon the foreign travel of its citizens. Even in open societies the encouragement or discouragement of foreign travel is done indirectly, through the regulation of air fares, currency restrictions, duty free buying limits, or diplomatic conditions.

By contrast the efforts to promote travel into one's country are becoming increasingly open and commercial. The developed countries are spending growing amounts on advertisement abroad, as are many developing states. In both kinds of economies the major thrust is made in the high income countries where the returns on investments of this nature are the highest.

The U. S. government is more involved today than ever before in trying to attract foreign visitors. Because Americans spend more abroad than foreigners spend in the United States, a deficit of about $3 billion on this travel account continues to remind U. S. government officials of the need, as they see it, to promote more foreign travel to the United States.

The governmental department to which this task has been assigned is the Department of Commerce. The International Travel Act of 1961 created within that department the United States Travel Service (USTS) whose primary purpose is to encourage foreign travel to the U.S. It is funded each year by the Congress, but the level of such support has become a mild political issue. Those in the USTS and groups within the travel industry strongly seek a larger budget. Perhaps their strongest argument for increased expenditure is that "In 1975, that return on investment ratio is expected to reach 10 to 1." [17] For every dollar spent by USTS on travel promotion in 1975, an estimated $10 would be earned by the United States in the form of tourism receipts.

In 1975 the USTS maintained 116 permanent positions with $11,250,000 appropriated for salaries and expenses. The concentration of expenditure and effort has been in six countries: Canada, Mexico, United Kingdom, France, West Germany and Japan. According to USTS this marketing strategy is based upon the fact that these six countries provide about 89% of foreign visitor arrivals to the U. S., about 74% of total tourism receipts, and 64% of the *potential* travel to the U. S. from the entire world (see Table 10).[18]

In 1975 Congress gave the USTS authority to promote domestic tourism with an appropriation of $2.5 million for each of the following three fiscal years. At the same time the USTS was authorized to spend $30 million each year for three years on its foreign programs. This legislation was strongly supported by the travel industry as well as by state and local governments whose economies were heavily tourism-oriented.

TABLE 10

Arrivals and Receipts from Six USTS Market Countries, 1974

	Arrivals (thousands)	Receipts (millions)
Canada	8,600*	$1,221
Mexico	1,841	873
Japan	763	434
United Kingdom	450	131
Germany	296	138
France	166	76
Total (USTS Markets)	12,116	2,873
Total (All countries, including transportation)	14,059	4,682
Total (All countries excluding transportation)		3,857

* Estimated.

Source: USTS Office of Research and Analysis, *Tourism Landmarks in 1974.*

Metropolitan countries look at international tourism mainly in terms of its economic value, although occasionally lip service will be paid to the value of tourism to international relations. In the United States, tourism is estimated to be a $61 billion business supporting 4 million jobs; tourism ranks among the top three industries in 46 of the states. Receipts from international tourism in 1974 amounted to $4.6 billion and generated an estimated 310,000 jobs.[19] Such values as well as the values to various economic interest groups within the travel industry are usually given considerable ritualistic attention before Congressional committees considering expenditures on tourism. The social or political issues of international travel are rarely discussed.

In pursuit of these economic emphases, the USTS works closely with the travel industry in the United States. In particular the Discover America Travel Organization (DATO) represents the bulk of the industry and keeps constant watch over governmental affairs which affect the welfare of its members. In March 1975 during two days of Congressional hearings on appropriations to USTS, the line-up of witnesses included spokesmen from virtually every type of travel organization — airlines, hotels, credit card companies, and state and local tourism offices.[20]

Whenever Congress conducts hearings on tourism, only passing comment is made on American travel abroad. The emphasis is upon promotion of travel to and within the United States. Even if government spends money to promote domestic travel by Americans, that promotion is not expected to reduce the travel of U. S. citizens abroad, but rather only to increase the numbers of citizens who travel at all. Openly to discourage American travel abroad would appear to many as a compromise of democratic principles of government or as an admission to the world that such foreign travel has begun to hurt the economy of the world's richest nation.

For the same reason, policymakers and industry leaders alike are reluctant to seek legislation requiring Americans traveling abroad to patronize U. S. carriers, even though these same leaders may personally favor it. The industry benefits from both tourism to the U. S. and from the tourism of Americans in foreign countries. Airlines, agents, international hotels, and credit card companies can compete in both environments. But is it not politically proper to lobby for tourism abroad of Americans — that is, to encourage Americans to travel abroad — thereby increasing the tourism receipts for other economies. It is more patriotic to lobby government for greater attraction of foreigners to the U. S., thereby increasing the nation's tourism receipts.

In both capitalistic and competitive economies, however, governmental expenditure for promotion of tourism amounts to a type of subsidy to that industry within its borders There is little wonder, therefore, that the giants of the travel industry line up before congressional committees seeking the promotion of their livelihoods at taxpayers' expense. By the government's own estimate there is a flow of $10 into the U. S. economy for every $1 spent on tourism promotion by the USTS in its six target countries. As each $10 flows into the U. S., however, it is first distributed among the institutions of tourism in exchange for transport, food, lodging and other retail sales. Only subsequently is there a *trickle down* effect from tourism receipts generated by this government promotion. Perhaps the strongest benefit, other than to the industry, is derived by various levels of government which according to the USTS, collected about $340 million in taxes from foreign tourists' expenditures in 1974.

There is virtually unanimous industry support for increased U. S. Government expenditure in other industrial states for promotion of travel to the United States. These industrial spokesmen cite as their main reason for this support the economic importance of tourism receipts to the U. S. economy. Underneath that reason lie the profit motive and the individual interests of the many institutions of tourism.

The majority of the institutions of tourism in the U. S. derive their income from tourists' expenditures, whether they be made by foreigners or citizens Only the larger multinational companies in international tourism stand to gain from the travel of Americans abroad, and even these companies are highly dependent upon tourism expenditures in the United States. The Chairman of the Board of Trans World Airlines has stated that two thirds of his company's business is essentially domestic.[21] For an international carrier like TWA, which also owns a hotel corporation (Hilton International), increased travel to the U. S. would likely increase its revenues on both the international routes and on its domestic routes as well. For U. S. multinational firms involved in tourism the solution to the travel deficit of $3 billion is not to reduce American travel abroad, but rather to increase tourism receipts in the U. S. through promotion in other metropolitan states. This, combined with fewer Americans using foreign carriers, would be a reasonable approach to the problem.

The U. S. government has been pressured to spend more money on tourism promotion for yet another reason. It is frequently pointed out by industrial leaders that many other countries including some developing nations spend more on such promotion than does the United States. Twelve other countries spend more: Ireland spends $21 million; Canada spends $25 million; and the United Kingdom spends $12 million compared to $9 million by the United States in 1973. Some small states like Bermuda or the Bahamas allocate a significant percentage (as high as 10 per cent) of their national budget to tourism promotion.

Additionally, the U. S. government has been encouraged by industry and by many lower levels of government to increase its budget for tourism because of the expenditures within the U. S. by foreign governments on similar ventures. To illustrate, the USTS has estimated that in 1970 the United States spent only $150,000 for advertising in Canada while the Canadians spent nearly $5 million on such promotion in the United States.[22] It was further estimated that in 1970 foreign countries altogether spent about $20 million on advertising in the U. S. media to promote American travel abroad. Since 1970 the U. S. Congress has increased its appropriations for tourism promotion. In 1976 over $11.5 million was appropriated for international promotion along with $1.2 million for domestic tourism.

Conclusion

The major concern in this chapter has been to outline the important political issues and interest groups involved in the promotion of metropolitan tourism to other countries. As we have seen, however, the politics of international tourism in the marketplace is overwhelmingly dominated by governmental and industrial efforts to attract foreign travelers to the United States. This brand of tourism politics is relatively open, is discussed at some length in congressional hearings, and is unanimously supported by industrial and political leaders alike. There is little debate and little controversy. Everyone seems to agree that increased foreign tourism to the United States is a good thing. We must have it! The only opposition to larger promotional budgets has come from the executive branch where the chief concern has been to hold the line on overall federal spending. In an economic sense the values of tourism have seldom, if ever, been questioned.

On the other hand, the politics of outward tourism from the United States are by far a more subtle process. Unlike the promotion of inward-bound travel, American travel abroad requires no appropriation of funds by the Congress. But tourism abroad is supported indirectly by the U. S. government through the pursuit of other national interests. Air transport agreements with foreign governments may be negotiated out of belief that viable air transport is in one's national economic, commercial or military interest. Tourism can then be the beneficiary of such agreements. Further, the profit motives of private tourism institutions can be served (favorably or unfavorably) by governmental pursuit of these larger national interests abroad.

Historically, and by comparison to most other states, the United States has not tried seriously to discourage travel abroad. It has forbidden travel by its citizens to certain countries with whom no formal diplomatic relations existed at that time. Yet, efforts to place other kinds of impediments on U. S. foreign tourism have always been met with hostility by strong interest groups. In the later years of his administration President Johnson, faced with a severe balance of payments problem, considered instituting a tax on foreign travel. He also considered reducing the maximum of duty-free purchases which could be returned to the country. However, he was immediately bombarded by pressure from an assortment of interest groups including the travel industry, and the entire approach was abandoned.*

The issue of American foreign travel has continued to be ignored.

---

* Johnson did appoint a task force in November 1967 to study ways to reduce the growing deficit in travel accounts and to increase foreign travel to the United States. The task force reported back that "The most satisfactory way to arrest this increasing gap is not to limit American travel abroad but rather to stimulate and encourage foreign travel to the United States."[23] The report listed some 26 actions or recommendations which could substantially increase the numbers of foreign visitors. The suggestions ranged from reductions in air fares and hotel charges to waiving of visas and streamlining the immigration and customs inspections. In its revised report, however, the task force ignored entirely the issue of American expenditure abroad. Instead it represented an overwhelming drive to make travel to the U. S. as cheap and as convenient as possible.

Congressional staff members cannot recall that anyone has raised the issue since President Johnson's suggestion in 1968 that American travel should be discouraged. Practically everyone in government is aware of the travel deficit, but no one seems willing to attempt to reduce that gap by endorsing governmental policy which would hinder the freedom to travel abroad. Instead, programs have been encouraged among local and state governments which would promote both increased domestic tourism and increased foreign tourism to the United States. In addition to its foreign operations the USTS has made grants available to various states and cities for the cost of advertising in foreign areas.

There is a mounting effort to offset the losses caused by foreign travel and expenditures of U. S. citizens by increasing tourism spending at home. In both the domestic and foreign markets this is being done through media advertising, offering attractive package plans and fringe benefits. The private sector is incrementally being aided in this task by public expenditure. Virtually no opposition has developed against this trend because the economic gains of such federal involvement in tourism have been repeatedly highlighted.

The United States government is committed to improving its position in world tourism. In addition to increased expenditure on travel promotion, the major thrust of this commitment is found in plans to establish a national tourism policy and to tighten federal coordination of tourism programs. Although such a recommendation was an output of President Johnson's task force in 1967 and 1968, the plan was not effected. As late as the fall of 1975 the Senate Committee on Commerce announced that the committee "will begin a National Tourism Policy Study under the direction of Senator Daniel Inouye (D.-Hawaii), Chairman of the Subcommittee on Foreign Commerce and Tourism." [24] The study had been authorized during the 93rd Congress by Senate Resolution 347, adopted unanimously by the Senate and sponsored by 71 senators. The intent of the study would be to produce a unified federal policy for the planning, development, and promotion of tourism in the United States. In the policy realm of tourism the United States is still a developing nation. As Senator Inouye has observed, "To my knowledge the United States is the only major country in the Western world that does not have a coordinated national tourism policy with some degree of centralized responsibility." [25]

Federal attention to tourism along with general economic stress has improved the deficit situation which has worried policymakers for so long. In 1974 U. S. receipts from foreign tourists increased by 17.3% over 1973 while expenditures increased by only 9.1%.[26] In aggregate terms, however, the United States continues to be the largest tourism generator and receiver in the world. The chief concern of tourism politics is the role of nations as tourism receivers.

In tourism, as in other economic activities, the metropoles of the world strive to be both the sender and the receiver. Metropolitan business strives to capitalize on the reality of metropolitan travel abroad and at the same time to profit from foreign travel to the homeland. In both ventures the assistance of government, if not entirely essential, is highly desirable. The metropolitan states are indeed the marketplace; it is there that tourists are bought and tourism is sold, where the geese get into formation. The host country, if it is not also a metropolitan one, may discover that the politics of tourism in the marketplace determines *who gets what*.

NOTES
Chapter 2

[1] OECD, *Tourism Policy and International Tourism in OECD Member Countries* (Paris: OECD 1974), p. 51.
[2] *ASTA Fact Sheet,* p. 1.
[3] For example see William E. O'Connor, *Economic Regulation of the World's Airlines* (New York: Praeger, 1971), pp. 94-107; and Mahlon R. Straszheim, *The International Airline Industry* (Washington: The Brookings Institute, 1969), pp. 8-30.
[4] The White House, *Statement of International Air Transport Policy, 1970.*
[5] According to *Aviation Week and Space Technology* (July 7, 1975), p. 25.
[6] Reported in *Aviation Week and Space Technology* (August 4, 1975), p. 31.
[7] Quoted by Robert Oppenlander of Delta Airlines in *Aviation Week and Space Technology* (April 7, 1975), p. 7.
[8] *Ibid.*
[9] *Aviation Week and Space Technology* (October 21, 1974), p. 24.
[10] *U. S. Statistical Abstract, 1974,* p. 215.
[11] *Vital Speeches* (June 1, 1974), pp. 506-509.
[12] See *Air Trans News* (June/July, 1972).
[13] Blaine Cooke, Senior Vice President for Marketing, TWA, in *Vital Speeches,* op. cit.
[14] See *Aviation Week and Space Technology* (October 6, 1975), p. 27.
[15] *New York Times* (May 28, 1975).
[16] *Aviation Week and Space Technology* (April 28, 1975), p. 32.
[17] Statement of Hon. Langborne Washburn, Asst. Secretary for Tourism, U. S. Congress, House, Subcommittee of the Committee on Interstate and Foreign Commerce, *Hearings HR 4449,* 94th Cong., 1st Sess., 1975.
[18] USTS Office of Research and Analysis, *Tourism Landmarks in 1974.*
[19] *Ibid.*
[20] *Ibid.*
[21] *Ibid.,* Statement of Charles C. Tillinghast, Jr., Chairman of the Board of Transworld Airlines, Inc.
[22] See the National Tourism Resources Review Commission, *Destination USA,* vol. 3 (Washington: U. S. Government Printing Office, 1973), p. 21.
[23] *Report to the President of the United States from the Industry Government Special Task Force on Travel, revised* (Washington: U. S. Government Printing Office, April 1968), p. 8.
[24] Press release dated November 3, 1975.
[25] *Ibid.*
[26] OECD, *Tourism Policy and International Tourism in OECD Member Countries 1975* (Paris: OECD, 1975), p. 76.

3
THE DEVELOPING HOST COUNTRY

We now turn to a brief study of tourism politics in that developing region which claims more American visitors than does any other part of the so-called Third World not contiguous to the United States. That Americans are mostly inclined to holiday in Europe as an overseas destination we have already noted. But aside from the adjoining states. Canada and Mexico, most other American travelers visit the West Indies. There, several small island countries have highly developed tourism industries. Tourism is highly visible, and highly *Americanized*. The Caribbean is the most popular Third World destination for American tourists other than Mexico.

Barbados has developed a large tourism sector even though it is a small island with only 166 square miles of land and 250,000 inhabitants. Tourism is its most important industry, surpassing sugar cane ever since 1973. It has nearly as many visitors per year as it has permanent residents. In 1974, over 230,000 foreign tourists arrived in Barbados; over 70% came from the United States, Canada and the United Kingdom. Nearly 30% were from the United States. For these reasons the island represents a good environment for examining the politics of tourism on the receiving end. The process of attracting tourist dollars has generated political behavior among West Indian states as well as international politics with the metropolitan countries. As an economic activity tourism has provoked both competition and cooperation among various Caribbean peoples.

In studying the Carribbean we can learn also about the effects of tourism in other developing regions of the world. There is a continuing controversy over the *real* value of tourism. Does it promote lasting development for the host country? Are the benefits derived spread out among the host population or do they remain with foreign investors and local elites? In other words, does metropolitan tourism into the Caribbean add wealth to the host country or merely to the metropolitan economies? How differently do political interest groups interpret the value of tourism to development?

Foreign tourism in the Caribbean also raises questions of cultural damage. Many perceive the foreign tourist to be a pervasive source of social, moral, psychological and racial frustration. If tourism is damaging to the host culture, what should host governments do about it? What is to be done, if anything, to ameliorate these effects? Should tourism be discouraged or perhaps eliminated altogether? These two controversies led to a cluster of political considerations concerning tourism.

A similarity between the politics of tourism in developing and metropolitan societies is found in the emphasis upon governmental policy which will increase national receipts from the industry. This is the major concern of tourism politics in most countries. However, a significant difference in the two kinds of societies may be found in the degree to which some interest groups in developing regions question the kind and level of tourism growth. In the large and wealthy metropolitan areas there are few if any challenges to such growth; but in small countries tourism can be a highly visible and highly threatening activity. It can be at the same time a lucrative one, forcing local peoples to make difficult choices between increased income and modernization on the one hand and cultural integrity and tradition on the other. Such choices have never been so pressing upon metropolitan populations. The recent tourist invasion of Great Britain has produced local resentment, however, attributable in some measure to population pressure and inflation.

The visibility of tourism and tourists in developing regions also contributes to the politicization of the industry. Visibility increases through contrast. In the Western metropolitan areas, for instance, most tourists are white and so are their hosts. On the other hand, most developing populations are dark-skinned, but play host to white North American or European travelers.

Further visibility through contrast is caused by the implantation of metropolitan institutions and services into developing nations. Luxury hotels, cruise ships ablaze with lights, and sleek jet airliners seem simply out of place alongside the dire poverty in many regions. Visibility through contrast serves to stimulate political and ideological resentment to the whole idea of tourism in the host, underdeveloped society.

The Development Issue

In the Caribbean, there has been a long and continuing debate over the value of international tourism to overall social, political and economic development. As an industry, tourism is a major source of foreign exchange earnings while at the same time it generates employment and governmental revenues. Yet, the central question continues to be whether these immediate benefits are shared by the entire host society or are merely restricted to those few people connected more directly with the tourism sector.

In the eastern Caribbean this argument crystallized in 1970. A study of tourism in that region by an American firm, Zinder and Associates of Washington, D. C., indicated that for every $1 spent by a tourist, about $2.30 would be generated within a given economy.[1] This *multiplier effect* was challenged by two economists at the University of the West Indies; Kari Levitt and Igbal Gulati found that only $1.073 was generated by each tourist dollar.[2] In explaining this finding the researchers pointed out that tourism was still highly dependent upon imported goods and services. Further, it was suggested that international institutions such as the World Bank have been successful in brainwashing policymakers in developing nations into seeing tourism as more beneficial than it really is.

John Bryden concluded in 1973 that tourism is not necessarily good for development.[3] Although there are some economic benefits (employment, foreign exchange), the social costs can be high. There are changes in local consumer demands brought on by tourism's influences. Tourism, unless properly controlled through policy, will be *import prone* and will not necessarily promote local agricultural and industrial sufficiency. In 1974 H. Peter Gray began his economic analysis of tourism by writing:

> No one will dispute the ability of tourists, as a species, to irritate their hosts through sheer arrogant display of wealth and/or brazen disregard of their hosts' sensitivities and values. The poorer the host country and the greater the degree of reliance of the host economy on the export of tourism services, the greater the susceptibility of the hosts to these irritants is likely to be.[4]

Gray points out that in developing countries where the above situation is extreme, the development role of tourism will suffer unless policymakers restrict the number of tourists. Using data collected in the Zinder Report, Gray demonstrates that the incidence of *unfriendliness* to tourists is highest in countries where the ratio of tourist arrivals to resident population is highest. This situation in turn leads to a decrease in the quality of tourism services and hence to a decline in prices which tourists can be charged.

There are other critiques of the value of tourism to developing states. Most critiques of the value of tourism raise questions about ownership and control of the industry and how these affect development. Ownership of tourism institutions depends to some extent upon the kind of industry found in a particular economy. As Bryden has stated, "So long as growth in the industry is based on large luxury hotels, then it seems almost inevitable that ownership will remain in foreign hands."[5] Smaller hotels and guest houses are more likely to be locally owned. In Barbados all guest houses were locally owned in 1971 (see Table 11).

Foreign ownership of large hotels is more acceptable to host governments because of the large amounts of capital required and because of the need for international expertise when dealing with metropolitan visitors. In some cases public ownership is arranged while a major hotel corporation, such as Hilton International, may hold a management contract only. Yet, the visibility of expatriate firms in Caribbean tourism causes questions to be raised by political groups about the value of a tourism industry dominated by these

TABLE 11

Ownership of Hotels in Barbados, By Type, 1971

Type of Property	Number Locally Owned	Number Foreign Owned	% Locally Owned
Luxury	3	10	23
Class A Hotels	3	8	27
Class B Hotels	6	5	55
Class C Hotels	2	1	67
Apartment Hotels	20	12	63
Guest Houses	10	—	100

Source: *Tourism Supply in the Caribbean Region* (Washington: The World Bank, 1974), p. 9. Based on a survey of C. Crocco.

large foreign institutions. Foreign ownership of a hotel suggests that profits will be repatriated and that the hotel's operation will be consistent with foreign values and practices rather than regional ones. In this manner the ownership question becomes a common point of debate in developing areas where tourism is deemed important.

Labor unions and radical groups in the Caribbean have been persistent in their warnings that foreign ownership of major institutions means less development for the host population. Their warning is countered by management, investors and local elites with the argument that metropolitan institutions are the key link with the world's tourism marketplaces, and that some foreign ownership, especially of luxury hotels, is desirable for reasons of market connection, expertise, and capital acquisition. In Barbados, for example, there have been no major political party differences on the matter of hotel ownership, although the Barbados Labour Party has urged that investments in small hotels and condominiums be reserved for local persons. Both major parties have leaned in that direction. Many small developing nations with limited territory have imposed strict limitations on foreign ownership of land.

Related to the question of ownership is the issue of control of the tourism industry in the host country. Ownership and control are not synonymous. Caribbean tourism is dependent upon a supply of North American and European visitors. The flow of these visitors is controlled by metropolitan institutions which *choose* to send them to the Caribbean rather than to some other destination. This is done through marketing devices: package sales made possible by wholesalers and tour operators who can pull the plug of Caribbean tourism at any time. This means that Caribbean tourism as a whole is controlled by external actors including foreign airlines, tour operators, major hotel firms, and others. Within the Caribbean small hoteliers must rely upon governmental tourism promotion in the metropolitan markets or conduct a modest campaign of their own. Both the small hotels and the luxury hotels cater to the metropolitan visitor, but the local ones have less representation in the North American or European marketplace.

If tourism is to serve development, can foreign control of the industry be tolerated? Is there a choice for Third World Countries? To some extent, *no*. For the foreseeable future the world's tourists will continue to be from the metropolitan countries where personal income is high. As we saw in the previous chapter even the urban countries invest their promotional funds in other urban states. Developing countries, which in 1968 had only 8% of the world's tourist arrivals and 20% of its receipts, must continue to rely upon a flow of metropolitan visitors who are processed by sellers in the developed states.

One of the major observations throughout the literature of tourism and development is that the industry in developing regions is prone to utilize imported goods and services. From a managerial point of view it is often cheaper to import when considering availability and product quality. But if tourism is to serve general development goals, the industry must be integrated into other local activities such as agriculture, fishing, and manufacturing. That is, local or regional products must be encouraged, and at the same time dependable supplies of these products must be developed if regional gains from tourism are to be maximized.

In the Caribbean other efforts have been undertaken to increase the developmental functions of tourism. Countries with large tourism sectors have acquired their own international air carriers as one way to increase tourism receipts. Although in some ways the ability of small states to operate airlines is extremely limited, it is a method of reducing external control of tourism. Similarly, efforts to bring other tourism institutions under national control result in a tightening of the bond between tourism and development. Banking facilities are essential to tourism, but they have often been accused of serving the needs of metropolitan actors and tourists in the developing nation rather than the needs of the host population. It is the responsibility of national governments to see that foreign banks establish practices to serve the needs not only of tourists or foreign managers, but of the residents as well.

Developing host countries can attempt to alter the tourist's experience in such a way as to increase the national benefits. This idea will be expanded in the next section, but its relevance to development cannot be overlooked. International mass tourism has operated on the model of simulation of metropolitan comforts while being in a foreign land. This is the major reason why tourism has been *import-prone* in developing regions. Localization of tourism would mean greater utilization of local talent, goods, and beauty, thereby increasing the contribution of tourism to societal development. As one example of the localization of the industry, Tapia House, a Trinidad-Tobago group, decided that there was no reason to have a Swiss chef in the Trinidad Hilton or souvenirs of the country made in Hong Kong.[6] Localization would not only reduce this dependence upon foreign items and reduce monetary leakage, but it would create a meaningful experience for the tourist by putting him in greater contact with the host culture. Managers of luxury hotels may say that all this sounds good, but that in reality their clientele consists of international people who desire a certain amount of standardized quality in service and accommodations. Other societies have begun to face up to this issue. As the Minister of Tourism in Fiji has put it, "We shall begin by looking inward towards the needs of our own society, rather than outward towards the capricious desires of a transient group."[7]

Finally, the Caribbean is increasing its control over tourism through a regional organization. The Caribbean Tourism Association undertakes marketing and advertising campaigns in the metropolitan countries independent of other private actors such as the airlines and hotels. The primary purpose of the CTA is to promote development of its member states through tourism. Such a purpose inherently means that CTA advertises on behalf of states, but at the same time it tries to sell the region as a whole, stressing the diverse attractions available to the visitor. Critics of CTA complain that it over emphasizes the commercial approach to tourism and that it virtually ignores the social and cultural stresses imposed upon the host populations by tourism. Nevertheless, the CTA represents a move by regional members to reduce their dependence upon other actors for tourism promotion in the metropolitan regions. As reorganized in 1975, the new CTA amounts to an umbrella association. It coordinates all regional tourism efforts including those of the Caribbean Hotel Association, the Eastern Caribbean Tourist Association, and the Caribbean Tourism Research Centre.

By its own admission CTA is primarily concerned with the marketing of Caribbean tourism destinations. It has not made any serious effort to question the effects of mass tourism upon host societies including any analysis of developmental impact. Presumably, the

Caribbean Tourism Research Centre will eventually include such concern among its projects.

George Young has listed five reasons why countries promote tourism: (1) tourism is a source of foreign exchange; (2) it is a growth industry; (3) tourism can exploit some competitive advantages (sunshine); (4) tourism can strengthen one's image abroad; and (5) employment.[8] Developed and developing countries alike see these as positive contributions to development. Too, there are social and psychological reasons why many people in developing regions promote tourism development. Some of these reasons are seldom admitted or they are subconscious. The desire to create symbolic institutions of modernization — high-rise hotels, swimming pools, airports — often overshadows the desire to alleviate poverty.

There are also some dangers in the large scale promotion of tourism. Inflation is one. The inclination of visitors to pay higher prices for goods and services leads to higher prices for everyone. The tourism infrastructure is expensive and must be paid for out of government revenues. In some small countries with no major exports, the economy can become too dependent upon a single activity controlled by external forces.

It is not the purpose of this chapter, however, to review the entire issue of tourism and development, but rather to stress that the development debate is an integral part of the politics of tourism in developing host countries. Many political interest groups construct an elaborate rationale for the growth and development of the industry because in their view tourism is good for the country. Other groups, especially those with populist qualities, tend to focus their attention on tourism development in terms of *who gets what*. As we shall see in the following chapter, the answers to *who gets what* in tourism may be preconceived by some as a result of their own ideological constructs and biases.

The Cultural Issue

In addition to the development question, a second important impact of tourism on host countries is the issue of cultural conflict. Especially where tourists and tourism stand in stark contrast to the host society, there is a high potential for cultural conflict. In many poor countries there are persons and groups who see the tourism intrusion as a threat to national identity, as an imposition of foreign values and tastes upon the host society. The intrusion of affluence begins with the establishment of corporate beach heads in prime holiday regions, leading quite expectedly to the institutionalization of metropolitan tastes in the host country.

The intrusion of corporate tourism does not in itself mean cultural conflict, but does, in the eyes of its critics, lead to it. The corporate managers begin immediately to develop work habits among local employees based upon metropolitan standards, but without the rewards of metropolitan wages and benefits.

The arrival of the metropolitan tourists themselves increases the potential for cultural conflict. They display affluence in poor countries. In the Caribbean white visitors are conspicuous even if they try not to be. They often pursue the four s's of tourism — sun, sea, sand, and sex — with an aggressiveness which seems grossly out of place in a casual Caribbean setting. They wear swimsuits to the supermarket and they make love on the beach. They demand loud rock music and rare steaks. Their local shopping is characterized by a single loud question: "How much is that!" Even when prices are ridiculously low some tourists feel compelled to argue.

Critics have observed that metropolitan tourists leave their morals and manners at home when visiting sun spots abroad. They seek exotic and erotic vacations far away from the social constrictions of their home. Members of host societies are expected to be servile. Although the behavior of some tourists may change completely between their home and destination, their expectations of material comfort remain the same or increase in their playground destination. Air conditioned rooms are required, familiar foods are demanded — both at the lowest possible price. Since the tourist has paid his fare, the host culture must now adapt to him.

Not all tourists, of course, are of this nature. In fact, most are not. But there are sufficient numbers who fit the above pattern to create cultural conflict. When complaints about tourists' behavior are lodged with host governments, officials are quick to ask the complaining residents not to judge all tourists by the distasteful actions of a few.

Unlike economic conflicts created by mass tourism, cultural conflicts appear to manifest themselves rather slowly. That is, the cultural issue does not enter the political system as quickly as does the issue of tourism and development. As a result of tourism in developing nations, cultural conflict is real, but it does not appear to be of pressing concern to local politicians. One reason for this is the populistic or cultural groups which are affected by this conflict have less political power than do the economic interests which promote tourism. This question will be discussed in greater detail in the following section on interest groups.

Cultural conflict created by mass tourism in developing countries continues to be a subject of political debate within host systems. Unfortunately, it is not frequently the topic of debate outside those host systems. Promoters of corporate tourism might improve their reception in host countries if they paid more attention to cultural diversity in such matters as management training.

Clusters of Political Interest

The politics of tourism in developing states can be analyzed quite fundamentally by identifying clusters of interests in tourism, by describing the respective memberships in each of these clusters, and by observing if possible the various ways in which these groups pursue their political interests. Important to this approach are the possible overlaps and defections from one group to another.

In Figure A the prominent clusters of political interest groups surrounding tourism are suggested. In most developing nations, and we think that this is particularly true of the Caribbean, tourism interest groups fall into four major clusters: (1) each national government; (2) the tourism industry, especially the managers; (3) local business and professional elites; and (4) populist groups including churches and labor unions. Most political behavior related to tourism occurs on behalf of members of one or more of these clusters. And, as we shall discuss later, membership and loyalty may involve a given person in more than one of these interest clusters.

National government. — Let us begin our four-part assessment of tourism interests in Barbados and the Caribbean by looking at the most pervading group — national governments. In developing regions, if tourism is to serve the national interest in some way, it becomes the responsibility of government to see that optimum benefits are derived. Governmental programs designed to achieve this objective are held up for public criticism by the other three groups as well as by the formal party opposition. Government's interest in tourism is simple in terms of purpose, but rather complex in terms of method. Its purpose, of course, is to orchestrate tourism policy in such a mnnner as to *maximize* national benefits from the industry. This includes decisions about how much foreign expertise or capital is *needed* compared to how much government feels should be *allowed*. How much revenue and of what kinds can be derived from tourism without scaring both the tourist and the investor away?

FIGURE A
Major Interest Group Clusters: Tourism Politics in Developing Countries

Populist Groups
unions
churches
universities
cultural groups
other political parties

Local Elites
business
professional
intellectuals

Government
National
Ruling Party
Opposition
Third Parties
Individual Officials

Tourism Industry Managers
expatriate managers
local investors
local labor

The methods of achieving this rather simple purpose, however, are quite complicated. Government, as an interest group, must pursue this general goal through detailed policies at the national, regional and international levels. It must negotiate air transport agreements with foreign states, including regional members, while simultaneously monitoring the business practices of local hotels, taxi operators, and storekeepers.

As we discussed in the earlier chapters, host countries, even very small states like Barbados, frequently perceive that they need a national airline in order to capture a share of the tourism transport market. Such an ambition might be rationalized in terms of needed foreign exchange earnings, but the profitability of such an airline may never be realized partly because of competition with better-operated metropolitan carriers. The Barbados government, for example, has struggled since 1974 to obtain routes for its designated carrier, ICA, into the United States. The U. S. Civil Aeronautics Board has refused such routes because it believes that ICA is not managed and operated by Barbados as a truly national airline.

This conflict, which exemplifies the interests of a host national government, took a new turn in 1976. Mainly because of the United States' denial of entry to International Caribbean Airways, the government of Barbados in March 1976 reduced the operating permits of two U. S. carriers to a duration of only three months.[9] Such action created unstable planning conditions for Eastern Airlines and American Airlines which serve the island's tourist flow from North America. Eastern had earlier been denied the right to carry pasengers between Barbados and Trinidad-Tobago. Regional airline spokesmen, including representatives of BWIA, attribute both of these actions by the Barbados Government to the struggle for ICA's entry into the United States.

Airline politics also illustrate the regional interests of national governments in tourism. While the government of Barbados has tried to obtain part of the North American travel market by promoting ICA as a national carrier, it has at the same time been in conflict with the government of Trinidad-Tobago, which has long promoted its carrier, BWIA, as a regional airline. Trinidad and BWIA have for years tried to convince regional governments that the most feasible approach to air transport in the eastern Caribbean would be for each government to support BWIA financially rather than to develop additional, competing carriers.

In its efforts to maximize national gains from tourism, a host government must occasionally use its power to discourage commercial practices which would reduce the national benefits. In 1971, for example, the government of Barbados discovered that certain hoteliers in the island were effectively circumventing currency controls and taxes by selling coupons abroad which could be exchanged for goods and services while visiting Barbados. Prime Minister Barrow said that these hoteliers were "like wolves descending upon the fold" and that they were taking advantage of the tolerance of the Barbadian people.[10] This practice could have enabled hotels with foreign connections to "sell Barbados" abroad without the host government being able to tax the sale. In a sense, it was a denial of the sovereignty of a host country. Foremost, however, this incident along with several others illustrates the frequent political conflict between national governments and managers in the tourism industry, especially expatriate managers. As the *Advocate News* reported on one occasion with respect to a proposed 4% tax on gross receipts of hotels,

> Mr. Barrow said that the attitude and action of these hotel managers constituted a contempt of Barbados and of the Legislature whose view it was that this (tax) should not be passed on to the guests. And it was to be noted that in the existing Hotel Association, president after president was an expatriate.[11]

Expatriate workers have always been another source of conflict between the tourism industry and host governments in developing nations. Although the conflict is a real one, it often appears to be a scripted drama with officials making a lot of public noise about the matter because it seems incumbent upon them to do so. Demands are sent to the large hotels stipulating that work permits will be issued only after the unavailability of local talent is clearly demonstrated.

Government uses its political influence on work permits in several ways. Through the unions the hotel managers are encouraged to train local persons for virtually every job including some management duties. And whenever permits are sought for key expatriate personnel, managers are frustrated by the sluggishness with which the application is processed. A common complaint among expatriate hotel managers is that the work permit requirement is used by national governments to harass rather than to promote the tourism industry. As one Canadian manager put it, "How the hell can it take three months for the papers to get down the street and back?"

But if work permits are used to harass the tourism managers, it must also be conceded that these same managers must indeed be reminded at times that they are operating in a *host* country. Work permits are an authoritative way of saying that the needs of the host population must come first. In 1972 the Minister of Home Affairs in Barbados, Ramses Caddle, told the House of Assembly in his country that:

... Only Barbadian citizens have rights in Barbados. Foreigners are accorded privileges but these privileges can be revoked or varied at the will of the Barbadian people. The right of Barbadian people both white and black must take precedence. They cannot remain second class citizens in their own country.[12]

Caddle was addressing the Assembly on matters of work permits. He expressed concern that expatriates earned larger salaries and received far greater expense accounts than those afforded to local workers. He even criticized foreign missionaries who came to Barbados to save souls, and who seem to return again and again to save the same souls.

Political relations between host governments and the tourism sector can become strained on other matters. Taxation is the major issue since it includes attempts by government to maximize revenues from rooms, food and beverage, transport, and imported items. Hoteliers catering to an international clientele resist increased or excessive tariffs on *luxury items* such as exotic foods and liquor. Such tariffs, they feel, raise costs to the point of no return and discourage tourists from returning. Governments may see these taxes as added revenue and as encouragement to the industry to buy local products and to indigenize the industry.

In an economic sense, one might conclude that developing host countries spend inordinate amounts of time and energy promoting tourism development. Less concern is displayed by host governments for the social dimensions of tourism. In Barbados occasional and passing attention might be given to social conflicts arising from large scale tourism, but serious programs designed to reduce those conflicts are noticeably missing. The growing incidence of male prostitution, for example, has prompted public complaints from visitors and residents alike. Yet, as late as 1975 the Minister of Tourism frankly admitted that the problem had not really been studied. The Minister did distribute a colorful poster in the island urging visitors to dress appropriately for church and for shopping. Bikinis on Broad Street are offensive to most Bajans (see Figure B).

Barbados is now an island almost entirely dependent upon the industry.[13] Some political leaders now concede that the island has reached its saturation level of tourists and tourism institutions. If that is the case, then future tourism development can concentrate on quality rather than quantity of service. Government can begin to deal more effectively with the social, cultural, and political effects of the industry.

The tourism industry. — The second important political interest group in the host country is the industry itself, especially its managers. In many ways it is possible to view workers and local investors as part of this cluster of political behavior surrounding tourism, but those actors might best be described under other headings such as populist groups or local elites.

In the Caribbean, expatriate tourism managers are far less patient with the local political processes than are nationals in management positions. Expatriates are constantly pointing out the inconsistencies of government policies on tourism — that on the one hand government professes to support tourism growth and refinement, while on the other hand it imposes every conceivable obstacle to good tourism management. Managers complain that they have to deal with government on too many matters, some of which should be routinely handled but which instead often require the approval of high level officials including ministers. Such a practice not only requires more time for routine paperwork to be done, but more seriously it frequently injects politics into business transactions that are essentially non-political.

From the industry's point of view, the results of this highly personalized political process is that management must work harder and longer for less profit than in similar tourism ventures in developed states. For example, it is not uncommon in Barbados or in other Caribbean states for the general manager of a large hotel to go personally to the airport or to the docks to clear an item through customs. Such needless delays demonstrate, in management's eyes, that national governments are not really interested in facilitating a smooth operation of the tourism industry.

As an interest group, tourist managers are a source of helpful information to policymakers in host countries. They know the industry better than most other persons. And while their political struggles with host governments may often be seen as the *profit motive versus national interest,* the two concerns do not always conflict. Managers often suggest to national officials that certain practices would enhance tourism and at the same time benefit local residents. Greater efficiency in tackling environmental pollution is needed in most developing tourism destinations. In Barbados, for example, the newspapers have echoed the managers' belief that a government which is highly dependent upon tourism could do more to remove garbage from the streets and beaches. Managers in tourism-related businesses see government officials as generally lazy and unobservant in the establishment of priorities about tourism. As one airline executive commented in 1974, "The Barbados government is so busy patting itself on the back that it never gets around to doing anything for local business." It is a fair assumption, however, that tourism managers as a political interest group spend most of their time watching out for their economic well-being when confronted with changing government policy.

In 1970 the Barbados government imposed a 4% tax on the gross receipts of hotels, a levy which could not be passed on to the tourist. The action was resisted by industry managers and one major expatriate firm threatened to sue for breach of contract under general principles of international law. Subsequently, the gross receipts tax was replaced with a room tax which could be borne by the consumer.

Although tourism managers persistently complain about what government does not do for tourism, it is also apparent that the industry could contribute more to a smoothly operating industry. Managers are so consumed by the market dimension of tourism that they rarely give serious attention to the social, cultural or psychological effects of their own actions upon local people. Those companies and tour operators which promote low cost package tours to Caribbean islands are often the last to consider the social effects or the economic benefits to host societies of that brand of tourism.

In the Caribbean, large hotel corporations are able to transfer guests to other islands in the event of a strike at a particular property. Such flexibility does exist, but is it never a first choice of action for managers who would prefer to continue business as usual. Yet, as multinational firms, some tourism institutions can try to accommodate their guests rather than lose them. Indeed, airlines and hotel companies have the advantage of expertise when dealing with host governments. In many small, developing, tourism destinations, political leaders try to play too many roles. They want to be politicians and legal negotiators at the same time. As a result tourism institutions often enter a country on rather lucrative terms. Host governments then attempt each year to rectify their mistakes in the initial negotiations.

It seems almost inevitable, therefore, that more stringent political controls will be placed on tourism in the Caribbean, if for no other reason than because the industry is so dominated by metropolitan corporations. Although external capital is needed, expatriate management and repatriated profits do not jibe with rising nationalism or with many new concepts of development. The tourism industry is today more than ever before being subjected to the question of *who gets what?*

Local elites. — The growth of mass tourism in Barbados and the rest of the Caribbean has benefitted some residents more than others. Business and professional elites have tended to welcome a growing tourism industry for obvious reasons: real estate values increase and demands for professional services increase as metropolitan institutions bring mass tourism to a developing region. Lawyers, physicians, real estate and insurance brokers all seem to gain from the presence of a significant tourism industry. Additionally, of course, most retail sales and services are available to the tourist and resident alike.

Other kinds of elites tend to challenge tourism more than do business and professional elites. In doing so they assume a basically populist stance. These populistic elites include several professional types of people: education elites, church leaders, labor leaders, and to some extent communications elites such as newspaper editors. There are other elite critics of tourism who may not be strongly identified with any of the above occupational groups: artists, writers and cultural leaders with varied backgrounds and interests.

There are several reasons why business and professional elites support large scale tourism in their own country. As mentioned earlier, the obvious reason is the profit to be earned from increased land values, increased demands for retail goods and professional services. A local physician might treat three tourist-patients at a luxury hotel and take in fees equal to a long day's work in his local clinic. Likewise, local lawyers are frequently the beneficiaries of the tourism intrusion since hotels, airlines and banks all need evidence of local representation on a day-to-day basis. And by comparison to fees earned from local clients, these resident legal elites receive handsome retainers from the expatriate firms. For these reasons one does not encounter or expect severe criticism of mass tourism among local professional elites.

Some mild criticism does come forth. Local business elites question the value of certain kinds of mass tourism. The inclusive tour charter (ITC) in their view brings to the host country a type of tourist who spends little in addition to the package of hotel and air fare. This kind of tourist frequents the fast-food outlets, eats hamburgers in his room, and perhaps buys two shirts made locally. The major economic gain from this usually summer visitor goes to the wholesaler or to the tour operator who likely lives in the metropolitan country, while the disadvantages are borne by the host society.

Local business elites also see the average ITC visitor as having poor taste in addition to a poor budget. He is not an experienced traveler and does not realize as readily as the winter visitor that host societies deem some pattern of dress and behavior as unacceptable. In Barbados a businessman noted that he had seen "this type of visitor sitting in the lobby of the Hilton in his underwear listening to a transistor radio."

Such impressions of the ITC tourist are shared by host government officials as well as other local elites. The Minister of Tourism in Barbados has on several occasions questioned the economic value of tour charters to his country. Business elites and officials agree, however, that a certain amount of ITC tourism is necessary for the overall industry, especially during the slack summer months when otherwise many hotel rooms would be empty.

Some local elites not directly tied to the tourism industry are able to benefit from its growth, yet at the same time to be critical of aspects of its development. Perhaps the best examples are communication elites. Local publications, especially newspapers, receive considerable advertising revenue from the hotels, airlines, banks and restaurants. Nevertheless, many editors and columnists do speak out on tourism issues, sometimes supporting the *status quo,* at other times challenging it. Some of the most vociferous observations about tourism-related behavior have appeared in the columns of Caribbean newspapers. In Barbados the *Sunday Advocate News* (August 4, 1975) ran an editorial entitled "Leave the Women Tourists Alone." The article deplored the increasing molestation of women tourists by local males including taxi men, waiters, and beachboys:

> It is a grave error to assume that every female visitor is coming to Barbados only to hop into bed with some *native* as part of her vacation experience.
> . . .
> Of course those who come to let down a bit more than their hair might welcome the opportunity, but again it is wrong to believe that all women are like that.
>
> It is perhaps inevitable that this type of behavior will surface whenever there is a tourist industry, but we cannot allow it to exist to the extent that it *creates problems for the industry.* (2nd italics mine)

While lamenting a particular problem in Barbados' tourism, the above editorial shows more concern for the effects of that problem upon the industry than upon the sensibilities of local residents. It was cast more in economic tones than in moral ones.

In the same month another Barbados newspaper, *The Nation* (August 10, 1975), carried a front page picture of a white female tourist attending the horse races in Bridgetown. The following caption reveals the editorial attitude (see Figure C):

> Horses are not the only attraction at the Garrison Savannah when the Barbados Turf Club's meeting takes place. The August meeting is no exception and this Ronnie Carrington picture captures all the attraction of *this close-fitting and skimpy outfit worn by a tourist last Saturday.* (italics mine)

People who publish newspapers might generally be part of the so-called commercial elite. But since most of their readers are local residents including industry and government leaders, they are more inclined to expose the maladies of tourism in the public interest. Besides, it makes good copy!

Other commercial elites are less willing to criticize tourism. Not only does their profiting from the industry keep them from opposing it, but their close identification with political leaders also explains a lot of their complacency. In most small Caribbean countries politics is a highly personalized activity — everyone knows everyone else and family histories are complex and interrelated. In short, while commercial elites find some aspects of mass tourism morally objectionable, they tend to pressure government only on economic matters pertaining to the industry.

Populist groups.— By definition, groups and individuals become populistic in their outlook on tourism whenever they show primary concern for the effects of tourism upon the total population of a society. Populism can be both a political goal and a political method. When analyzing tourism, populists want to know whether the industry benefits the average citizen who makes up the bulk of any society. Populism as a goal means that if tourism benefits only a few elites, then the industry must be changed or abolished. As a method, populism is the technique of promoting one's ideas or programs through broad popular acceptance of their content. The role of populism as a goal is perhaps more evident. The major emphasis is upon persons or groups who are asking critical questions about the effects of mass tourism upon the total host society.

There are many such groups. Among them the most important seem to be labor unions, churches, university academics, and some other cultural or political groups, including some new political parties. In the Caribbean, leaders of all these interest groups have leaned toward populistic analyses of mass tourism.

Labor Unions. — Of the four basic groups to be discussed, labor unions are by far the most concerned with the everyday fiscal dimensions of mass tourism. Wages and worker benefits are, of course, of prime importance. But union leaders also express apprehension about many effects of tourism upon the host society. They are concerned about the growing domination of tourism by large metropolitan firms, about the concomitant cultural intrusion, and about rising inflation brought on in part by events outside the host country

Recent events in Barbados provide a good case study of union dissatisfaction with segments of the tourism industry. In late 1973 negotiations between the Barbados Workers Union and The Barbados Hotel Association failed to produce agreement on wage increases for a new three-year contract. For some workers union demands amounted to as high as a 70% increase. Hoteliers refused to consider such high raises and on December 31 (in time for New Year's Eve clebrations) a strike began against luxury and Class A hotels. Table 12 indicates the union demands, the hotel proposals and the settlement figures for the dispute which ended on January 4, 1974.

In the course of events surrounding this strike in early 1974, the political attitudes of union leaders toward mass tourism became clear. Foremost was the notion that luxury hotels reap handsome profits for their foreign owners because they pay local workers a bare subsistence wage. A hotel maid earning $50 (Barbados) *per week* was likely cleaning rooms which rented for a high as $260 *per day*. Managers argued that the wage rates were compatible with the rest of the local economy and in some cases were higher for similar work in government or other industry. Union leaders viewed the issue differently. Their concern was that $50 per week even in Barbados does not allow one to live above a subsistence level. (This is about $25 U.S. or Canadian, per week.) On this issue the union had widespread support from various sections of the community and certainly from other populist groups.

TABLE 12

Wage Negotiations, Barbados Hotel Strike, 1974, Luxury Hotels*

Worker Category	Union Demand Increase	Settlement	Hotel Proposal
Earning $40 or more per week	$20 per week in 1st yr., $2 in 2nd year	$12 first year, $8 second year	$17 first year, $3 second year
Earning less than $40 per week	$15 per week in 1st yr., $2 in 2nd year	$12 first year, $4 second year	$14 first year, $2 second year

* Figures are in Barbados dollars. $1.00 Barbados equals about $.50 U.S.

TABLE 13

Selected Weekly Wage Rates, Luxury Hotels in Barbados, 1973 and 1975

	Barbados dollars*	
	1973	1975
Head Waiter	$53.50	$73.50
Bartender	53.50	73.50
Scrubber	—	46.00
Maid	34.00	50.00

* $1.00 (Bdos) = $.50 U. S.

The five-day strike had some curious features. At the Barbados Hilton, workers reported on time the first day, and as usual set up the dining rooms for breakfast. But when guests arrived, the workers refused to serve and obstructed management personnel who tried to arrange a make-shift buffet. At other luxury hotels similar incidents were reported. Workers did not merely picket; they wanted no food or beverage service to guests within the hotel. Minor incidents of violence were reported, but in general there was little threat to the safety of visitors. Frank Walcott, the General Secretary of the BWU, said to visitors at a public meeting during the strike that "every Barbadian considered himself a self-appointed policeman who loved nothing better than to conduct traffic."[14] In other words, visitors should not fear for their safety.

The political dimensions of the strike were more obscure than the clearly fiscal aspects. Members of government were careful not to take a public stand with either the union or the hoteliers. The union leader, Frank Walcott, was a member of the ruling Democratic Labour Party in the House of Assembly. Various members of the opposition Barbados Labour Party sided with the workers, pointing out that inflation had made higher wages necessary and that the DLP had done little to curb the rising cost of living in the island. Remarks made by the Prime Minister at various times during the strike reflected mainly a concern for safety of persons and property.

Public attitudes toward the 1974 hotel strike in Barbados might be separated into the following three basic positions: (1) a view that the union's demands were entirely justified for several reasons, including the oppressive cost of living and the belief that luxury hotels were exploiting local workers by paying bare subsistence wages while charging the tourists exhorbitant prices for rooms; (2) a view that wages paid by hotels were generally higher than wages for comparable work elsewhere in the island, and that the union demands were excessive beyond all reason in the context of the total economy; and (3) a belief that higher wages were greatly needed by hotel workers, but that a prolonged strike would do serious damage to the tourism industry and to the image of Barbados abroad.

Outside of Barbados, views were similarly divided, but perhaps with more evident concern for the plight of the tourists. Canadian newspapers published tales of disgruntled tourists who had spent as much as $3000 Canadian for an aborted, horrible experience at the (Canadian) Holiday Inn in Barbados.[15] One visitor described the Holiday Inn as a pigsty during the disorder, while others reported that guests were not terribly inconvenienced and that management personnel did an admirable job of helping guests care for themselves. One Canadian paper expressed mild shock over the wages paid by a Canadian firm in Barbados:

> It may be unfair to single out the Barbados Holiday Inn in trying to get a sense of proportion about this wage dispute. After all, it is one of the more pricey hotels. Nevertheless, it does seem to indicate something askew when the standard single room rents for $96 a day in Barbadian currency or $480 for a five-day week, and a worker earns $50 a week.[16]

There is no better summary of the concerns of the Barbados Workers Union. As the thoughts of its leaders on tourism have evolved over the years, so also has there been an increasing awareness of the role played by multinational business in the tourism sector. BWU General Secretary, Frank Walcott, said as early as 1972 that:

> All of the trade unions in the Caribbean have a duty to one another to see to it that the multinational corporations do not swallow up the society — lock, stock and barrel, by such power over the governments that they become stronger and more powerful than the elected governments of the respective countries.[17]

In Barbados Walcott has alleged that employers, especially the large hotel firms, have tried to use government in their efforts to control workers. In the 1974 strike employers' complaints about trespassing and other disorders were seen by Walcott as an attempt by managers to co-opt government — to force officials to accept the view that law and order must be maintained at all costs and that property rights are more important than workers' rights.

Wages and working conditions have not been the only interests of unions pertaining to mass tourism. Union leaders share with other populists the fear of cultural damage caused by imposing foreign values. For example, metropolitan visitors have always found it *quaint* that in the Caribbean most shops and businesses close at four o'clock in the afternoon. In Barbados supermarkets have customarily closed at 1 p.m. on Saturday and re-opened at 8 or 9 a.m. on Monday. But in 1975 the Government of Barbados proposed a Shops Act Bill to be considered by the House of Assembly. The bill would call for legal permission for shops to remain open into the evening hours and on Sunday. Supporters of the legislation saw added convenience to tourists and residents alike as the main goal. Although the measure provided for adequate controls on workers' hours and overtime pay, the union posed it:

> We are aware of the pressures that can be used to make Barbados conform to the whims and fancies of the tourists; but it must be remembered that the people who live in Barbados must matter and that the shop assistants have a right to protection against unscrupulous employers.[18]

Walcott felt that demands for longer shop hours had not been expressed among local people, that instead the proposed changes were the result of metropolitan values. He said, "They have brought Miami into Barbados and they will be bringing London next into Barbados."[49] He thought the proposed legislation would amount to additional exploitation of lower class workers by the tourism institutions. Walcott's views clearly contradict those of government leaders in his own majority party.

In Barbados union pursuit of tourism politics has been rather direct through party politics. The views of union leaders are routinely expressed on the floor of the House of Assembly. During the first decade of independence, the Barbados Workers Union enjoyed close identity with the ruling Democratic Labour Party of which the union's General Secretary was an elected Member in the House of Assembly. Thus, relations between the union and the Government have tended to be good as well as personal. Even so, the triangular relationship between the union, government and tourism management is often a curious one. While government and labor both are wary of the external control of tourism, government seems less militant on matters of wages and employment. It does not wish to see union activity jeopardize in any way the free flow of tourists' dollars upon which all are so dependent. Both labor and management suspect each other of trying to sway government officials toward their respective views of industrial relations. Neither seems to have been wholly successful and the game goes on. In September of 1976, the Barbados Labour Party regained control of the government. Whether that party adopts a fundamentally different tourism policy remains to be seen.

In summary, the political goals of union activity on tourism in the Caribbean are several. First, wages and worker benefits must increase drastically in light of the rising costs of living, even in

FIGURE B
Barbados Tourist Poster

other occasions. One might argue that even without tourism such discourse would take place in a country ringed with lovely beaches and a warm climate. But churchmen are now stressing that tourists wearing *skimpy outfits* have encouraged residents to do likewise. Newspapers in Barbados have explored the subject on many occasions.

Yet, dress habits have not been the most controversial moral issue. First place honors have gone to the general subject of *sex,* one of those four *s*'s of tourism. In Barbados, the broad subject of sexual behavior and tourism has been narrowed down somewhat, to one aspect which in the views of clergymen and others poses serious threats to tourism and the society. Barbados has earned a reputation in the Caribbean of having a well developed industry of male prostitution. The industry has a racial dimension in that it thrives on the alleged desire of white female tourists to have sex with black males. Attitudes have formed in the Caribbean and in metropolitan countries that racial curiosity among the visitors accounts for most of this behavior. An article by Robert Turnbull in a Canadian paper stated:

> Without exaggerating the situation, an amazingly large number of Canadian and American women, married and single, do travel to the Caribbean with black sex more their goal than a suntan. They get both. The women frequently arrive with introductions to specific beach boys from satisfied customers.[22]

The blame for this *immoral* conduct is most frequently placed upon the white visitor, although a general disdain for beach boys has also developed among Caribbean residents. Although homosexual relations have developed between black local males and white male visitors, little public discussion has taken place about the issue. The so-called *Canadian secretary syndrome* — that is, white female visitors in search of black local talent — has been the subject of most discussion.

There perhaps was a time when black male prostitution in Barbados tourism was confined to the beach boys, young males who hang out near luxury hotels displaying their bodies in view of white female tourists. But as the demand for service has increased with growing mass tourism, other occupational groups have sought a "piece of the action." Taxi drivers, waiters, bartenders and busboys have utilized their positions in the industry to make contact with arriving potential customers. An attractive English girl reported in an interview that "I was propositioned five times between Seawell airport and my hotel room. What shocked me was that two of them had professionally printed business cards. But they were all rather polite!"

Although there has been little serious study of this phenomenon

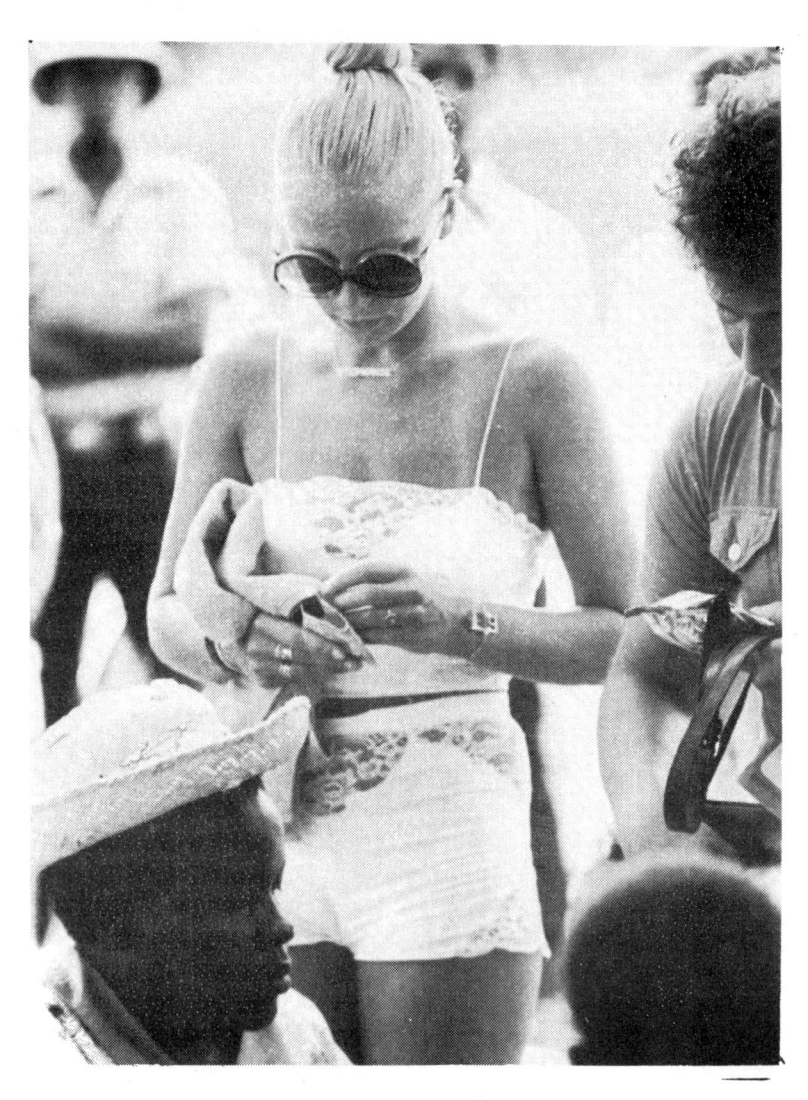

FIGURE C
Scantily Clad Tourist in Barbados

by social scientists, beach-chair psychologists have theorized at great length about it. The most common hypothesis is that women from America and Europe have fallen for the myth that black men are sexually well-endowed, and that in metropolitan societies white women seldom have the chance to get into bed with a black man. So, a visit to the Caribbean creates that opportunity free of the social constraints at home. Whatever the reasons might be, it is a fact that such activity has generated a thriving industry in the Caribbean. And it is not the kind of indigenous activity that the church leaders had in mind.

Many of the clergy feel that politicians are ignoring the problem. Prostitution creates related ills such as drug abuse, theft, pimps, and veneral disease. One clergyman has given an economic twist to the matter: "Between December 15 to April 15 we cannot find any able-bodied young men to cut sugar cane, even at $100 a week."[23] Beachboys who make a living from sex do not rely entirely upon being paid in cash. Frequently, they just share a hotel room with their client, enjoying good food, drink and dancing all at her expense for a 21-day excursion. Beach boys have been known to trade customers, bargaining for equity payments as part of the deal.

It is this latter behavior pattern that annoys hoteliers the most. If a hotel gets a reputation for such activity, other *boys* in search of business will appear, thefts and disorders increase, and other guests become dissatisfied with the social climate in the hotel. "It's bad for business," say hotel managers, "and government does little about it."

The thinking of moral leaders such as clergymen is not confined to tourism's influence upon sex or dress. According to some churchmen, tourism perpetuates a general feeling of colonial dependence and servility. Caribbean peoples have begun to overcome the effects of a long colonial experience only to find themselves confronted once again with white metropolitan visitors who display their affluence carelessly. The church's message to various governments is clear: integrate the tourist experience with the local experience. Make the goal of tourism a meaningful intercultural experience! Progress toward such a goal will require great effort on the parts of metropolitan governments, host governments, and certainly the industry managers themselves.

Academics and other groups. — There is considerable overlap of the views of clergymen and academics, especially on the matter of cultural effects of tourism. In the Caribbean most attention to mass tourism emanating from the universities has been of an economic nature. Like other populists, these thinkers are not opposed to all tourism. They are keenly interested in the refinement of the industry, particularly in terms of shifting more and more of the economic benefits from outsiders to local persons.

Owen Jefferson, an economist at the University of the West Indies, has expressed four major concerns for tourism-dependent societies in the Caribbean.[24] First, he observed that many economies had become too dependent upon an industry that is frequently an unstable one. Political unrest in one part of the Caribbean can reduce tourism in another part. Cuba's dependence upon American tourists prior to its revolution in 1959 meant that after the socialist revolution the entire industry virtually disappeared.

Secondly, Jefferson and other economists have noted that there is not enough retention of the economic value of tourism in the host country. Importation of goods and services remains too high. (See the discussion of work by Levitt and Gulati in the first pages of this chapter.)

Third, tourism adds to inflation in a number of ways. Local agriculture declines as tourism claims more land at high prices. Workers are drawn from the farming sector to the higher wages of tourism-related jobs. Prolonged exposure to foreign tastes and life styles results in greater demand among local residents for foreign-made items. More importantly, the earning gap between tourists and local people means that the visitor can pay higher prices for many of the same goods and services required by their hosts. Inflation increases.

Finally, economists and other social scientists object to the development of *enclave tourism* in host countries. Such enclaves have been called *white ghettos* by critical journalists who see the geographic separatism as symbolic of the social, economic and cultural disparity characteristic of highly institutionalized mass tourism today. While existing along side the host society, many of these resorts demand the best that the country can provide: the best beaches, the best goods, the best entertainment. These demands have led Neville Linton, a political scientist at the University of the West Indies in Trinidad, to see some Caribbean tourism as *whorism*. The tourist is seldom encouraged by the promoters to discover the real nature of host societies.

> This means for instance, that instead of the urbane pap which is put on tourist brochures one can imagine a piece like this: Barbados today is the result of 300 years of colonialism and 5 years of independence. What you see around you is the outcome of that process — a people struggling to establish an economy that can be beneficial to them; a young people proud of their culture about which we hope you will learn a bit during your stay. Barbados is not a beach — it is a new state struggling to make its contribution to a brave new world.[25]

Linton's critique of tourism stressed that the industry, if managed properly by host governments, could be "an activity of the highest utility." Jobs in tourism could be less demeaning than factory or agricultural ones and tourism offers many opportunities for mind-expanding employment.

Poets and playwrights have joined the social scientists in pointing out the synthetic quality of much tourism. Consider the following poem by Bruce St. John:

ART

> Painter pon de sidewalk,
> Painter at de Hilton,
> Painter in the country,
> Painter in town.
>
> Painter paint beach, beach, beach.
> Painter paint tree, tree, tree.
>
> Painter doan paint studyation
> Painter doan paint worryation.
> Painter don't paint the nation.[26]

Other populist groups are led by academic people, although the groups' approach to political activism might be more popularly based than academically inclined. In Trinidad, for example, Tapia House is considered a radical political activist group which on occasion has criticized the state of Caribbean tourism. In 1971 it urged regional states to return to a boarding-house tourism where visitors' tastes would be less exotic. Tapia also urged that travelers who have some cultural affinity for the region should be encouraged to come to the Caribbean. Black Americans or Canadians would constitute such a market.[27] Tapia's thesis was that such a brand of tourism would accomplish two things: (1) it could make tourism a culturally worthwhile venture for all concerned, and (2) it would increase the reliance of tourism upon local talent and resources, thus preventing monetary leakage.

More recently in Barbados new political parties have arisen which question the direction of tourism. Frank Alleyne, an economist at the University of the West Indies in Barbados, has stated that his Peoples' Democratic Movement sees six major policy questions in tourism:

(1) The failure to integrate tourism growth with development in agriculture.
(2) Tourism's competition with the farming sector for labour and capital resulting in a retardation of agriculture.
(3) What balance should there be between large hotels and small ones including guest houses?
(4) Training for tourism including training at the highest managerial levels.

(5) Ownership patterns of hotels.
(6) Development of the local environment for better use of leisure in Barbados.[28]

Other political groups in Barbados share Alleyne's views. In general their common concern centers around the need to refine tourism and the need to put greater emphasis upon the expansion of local agriculture and fishing. In their view the tourism sector has been allowed to develop too much on its own terms, importing a large portion of its foodstuffs and other requirements without due regard for stimulating local supportive activity. Blame for this lack of tourism control is placed upon the two major parties which have controlled the country prior to and since independence.

Conclusion

In examining Caribbean nations as examples of developing host countries in international tourism, it must be remembered that in that region tourism and tourism politics are considerably more advanced than in other parts of the Third World. Both the level and duration of tourism development have perhaps given rise to more political discussion of the industry than in other regions.

The Caribbean is a region of non-white populations whose visitors are mainly white metropolitan residents. Thus, as in the rest of the Third World, Caribbean mass tourism has a racial dimension. It is seen by some as a *white corporate intrusion* followed by a mass intrusion of white tourists seeking to enjoy their leisure away from the industrial centers of the north.

The visibility of tourism in the Caribbean in terms of race and affluence has added to the growing debate about the international activity. The cultural and economic gap between the visitor and the host led at one time to a *revolution of rising expectations* in the developing world, a hope and a belief that wealth would flow from the metropolitan states into the developing ones. More recently, it has become apparent that wealth is not shifting in favor of residents of the developing region and as a result there have been thoughts of a *revolution of sinking expectations*. That is, the economic benefits of international tourism have not been accruing to the developing states at a desirable rate. For both the developing host governments and their nationalistic critics the fundamental question continues to be *who gets what* from international tourism.

NOTES
Chapter 3

[1] Zinder and Associates, *The Future of Tourism in the Eastern Caribbean* (Washington: Zinder and Associates, 1969).

[2] Kari Levitt and Igbal Gulati, "Income Effects of Tourist Spending: Mystification Multiplied: A Critical Comment on the Zinder Report," *Social and Economic Studies*, vol. 19, no. 3 (September 1970), pp. 326-343.

[3] John Bryden, *Tourism and Development: A Case Study of the Commonwealth Caribbean* (Cambridge: At the University Press, 1973).

[4] H. Peter Gray, "Towards an Economic Analysis of Tourism Policy," *Social and Economic Studies*, vol. 23, no. 3 (September 1974), pp. 386-397.

[5] Bryden, *op. cit.*, p. 219.

[6] *Tapia* (August 29, 1971).

[7] *Tourism International Newsletter* (mid-July 1974), p. 3.

[8] George Young, *Tourism: Blessing or Blight?* (Middlesex, England: Penquin Books Ltd., 1973), p. 132.

[9] Reported in *The Nation* (Barbados), March 28, 1976.

[10] *Advocate News* (Barbados), March 25, 1971.

[11] *Ibid.*

[12] *Advocate News*, March 6, 1972.

[13] Nigel Barrow in *The Nation*, April 4, 1976.

[14] Statement of H. Peter Morgan, Minister of Information, 4th January 1974.

[15] See *The Star* (January 2 and 3, 1974), and *The Globe and Mail* (January 2 and 3, 1974).

[16] *Globe and Mail*, Januray 3, 1974.

[17] In a speech to the National Workers Union in Jamaica, cited in *Vanguard* (Trinidad), March 25, 1972.

[18] *Nation*, September 21, 1975.

[19] *Nation*, February 1, 1976.

[20] *The Role of Tourism in Caribbean Development* (Bridgetown: CADEC, n. d.), p. 18.

[21] *Ibid.*, p. 19

[22] *Globe and Mail* (Toronto), January 20, 1975.

[23] Roy Neehall, quoted by Turnbull, *Ibid.*

[24] A speech to a Tourism Month Seminar in Jamaica, reprinted in *The Jamaica Weekly Gleaner*, November 8, 1972.

[25] "Tourism and Race Relations: A Third World Perspective," a paper presented to the Caribbean Ecumenical Consultation on Tourism, 1971.

[26] In *Savacou* (December 1970/March 1971), p. 82.

[27] *Tapia*, August 29, 1971.

[28] Personal correspondence with the author dated November 11, 1975.

4
SOME BIASED PERCEPTIONS OF TOURISM

As already noted, the activities which prompt the flight of our tourist-geese evoke a range of feelings about the real nature of tourism. It can be seen on the one hand as a natural expression of man's freedom, and on the other hand as a monster of corporate capitalism, which continues to exploit nature rather than servicing it. These various perceptions of the same activity lead inevitably to social, economic and cultural conflict. We have already discussed some of these in the preceding chapter. More importantly perhaps, the conception of world tourism in the future will likely be the result of some combination of these views. It seems unlikely that nationalism in the Third World will allow tourism to remain so highly beneficial to the metropolitan states at the expense of developing nations. Too, it seems equally unreasonable to expect tourism to disappear as a profitable activity for corporate capitalism.

Most ideological debate about tourism starts from the premise that the basic cluster of activities which we call *tourism* is likely to continue in the foreseeable future. The debate is not so much concerned with tourism versus no tourism as it is with *what kind of tourism*.

Strong views are shaped by the dominant values, goals and experiences of a person or group. Not everyone has developed such views. For the average citizen in both the developing and the developed countries, tourism is not a subject commanding great philosophical thought. Yet, for some individuals — mainly elites in business, government or academic circles — many facets of tourism have become an obsession, often dominating their thoughts and feelings about the nature of man and about the future of the world in which we all live, work and play.

From those persons who have thought critically about world tourism one can hear a whole spectrum of political beliefs, ranging from those which denounce tourism as undesirable *per se* to those which see the industry as a new vanguard of international culture and brotherhood. Like political ideologies in general, these *systematic* ways of looking at tourism are also *biased,* resulting from a preconceived view of the nature of tourism as well as a preconceived notion about what the nature of tourism should be. And, like ideologies in general, each of these coherent views of tourism has something to offer to the others, even if the overall view is rejected. Indeed, contemporary world tourism reflects many perceptions of the same activity. All groups seek to actualize their ideas about tourism, and in doing so they contribute to the general nature of the industry at any particular time. Out of the differences of opinion will come, one might hope, a better understanding among people who have varying stakes in tourism activity. Can corporate or capitalistic interests be reconciled to the social or developmental interests in Third World nations? If so, what will be the nature of that new brand of tourism? Whose interests will it serve?

Tourism and metropolitan capitalism. — Capitalists have many beliefs which bear upon modern tourism. Among the most important is the view that man should be free to compete for his needs and wants. What is produced should depend solely upon demand. Further, the price of those goods and services which are produced will be determined by the willingness of buyers to pay. Government should not interfere with this basic process. Capitalists take pride in the fact that most international tourists today come from countries where a high degree of free and private enterprise has been maintained. They see this as evidence that the values of capitalism produce greater and not lesser freedom for the individual than will other types of economic systems. In their view, not only does capitalism increase man's freedom, but it also increases the means with which to enjoy that freedom — namely, surplus income and leisure. Thus, say the capitalists, international travel as a means of relaxation and human enrichment is best attainable under an economic system free of government restraint.

For the capitalist this freedom from government control also means that economic groups are free to organize for profit the foreign travel of fellow citizens. The world view of international tourism becomes for the capitalist a logical extension of his dominant values and goals. These include the freedom to compete for any reasonable profit in any tourism-related activity for which there is a demand. The fact that metropolitan residents are able to finance foreign holidays is sufficient incentive for others aggressively to provide for the requirements of the traveler. To capitalists, therefore, tourism becomes a commodity to be sold at a profit.

Tourism, in other words, is a market. It is a demand for labor, goods, and services. Like other economic activities in capitalistic societies, tourism has come to be dominated by corporate capitalism. Airlines, hotel chains, restaurants and credit card companies reflect the modern approach to production through large accumulations of capital (money). In corporate philosophy, if greater amounts of money are invested, greater profits will accrue. At the same time a wider choice of goods and services can be produced at a lower price.

Concurrent with the rise of corporate capitalism has been the reliance upon advertising as a means of creating markets. International tourism, like any other comsumptive process, can easily be manipulated by the advertising ability of corporations competing for a share of the tourism market. In a sense, world tourism is corporate tourism. The first flow of tourists into a new destination is usually preceded by corporate beach heads in those countries. Corporate managers maintain that they are responding to a new market demand, but in reality the new markets are created by the capitalists who, after an analysis of market potential, establish themselves in new host countries.

The role of advertising can be illustrated by the joint advertisements of airlines and hotels for packaged trips to certain destinations. In popular travel magazines and in leading newspapers one can observe the combined efforts of hotels like Holiday Inn or Hilton International and airlines like American or Eastern. When an airline and a hotel company serve the same destination, new markets can be created through their joint advertising campaigns. Which came first, the market (demand) or the supplier? Ideally, under capitalism the demand always precedes the supply, but modern capitalists have come to create through advertising demands for only that which it is their business to supply.

For these reasons the tourism industry provides a good study of modern capitalism in action. If the individual is free, as the capitalists would have it, then he is free to acquire material things and to expend his wealth on whatever he chooses. As capitalistic man is naturally aggressive, competitive and acquisitive, when he travels abroad he will demand many different goods and services. He will want to visit societies different from his own, but while doing so he will demand elements and symbols of his own culture. He may wish to visit Barbados, but he will prefer to go there on a modern jet, stay in a luxury hotel, and enjoy food, beverages and even entertainment imported from home. These are all traits which capitalists might ascribe to the typical foreign traveler.

However, one might ask, are these traits real or synthetic? Are the demands of the institutional tourist a consequence of his becoming used to a certain standard of living, or has corporate capitalism successfully conditioned him to expect certain amenities which he would not customarily experience at home?

Within a capitalistic view of tourism it is likely that the preceding questions would never be asked, for if all capitalists are really free individuals, they can choose to acquire only those goods and services which they genuinely want or need. Other persons are at the same time free to try to sell us goods or services which we do not want or need. If there is little demand for certain things, those items will cease to be plentiful. Thus, from a classical capitalistic perspective the high degree of institutionalization in world tourism today is the result of two basic things: (1) more and more tourists (especially from capitalistic nations) have increasing amounts of money to spend on travel and concomitant goods and services; and (2) if free from governmental constraint, institutions and individuals alike will increasingly compete to supply these new demands of world tourists. In actuality it is not important to capitalists how the new demand arises. What is important is that government, any government, not restrain the process described above. Tourism and all of its related economic activities should be the result of free men and women exercising their freedom, their earned leisure, by making many free choices.

This capitalistic attitude is not without merit. It says to all its critics that the crucial component of world tourism is the tourist. The traveler is a free agent. If he desires certain goods and services and is willing to pay for them, why should the suppliers of his needs be criticized for making a profit? Someone once remarked that prisons will never improve until they obtain a better quality prisoner! Is not the quality of tourism dependent upon the qualitative demands of the tourist? The whole chain of political, economic and social events which comprise the industry begins with the decisions of individuals to visit foreign lands. The fact that their decisions are connected directly to the options available to them or the fact that certain options are made more attractive than others does not negate the freedom of either the consumer or the supplier.

The preceding paragraph should not imply that there are highly structured views of tourism held respectively by capitalists and non-capitalists. What is stressed is that within corporate capitalism one finds a basic view of tourism as a cluster of economic activities which naturally result from man's freedom to compete in efforts to supply the demands of fellow world citizens. The social value of tourism becomes rather incidental or in some instances assumed. Socialist states, on the other hand, tend to reject the overproduction of tourism-related goods and services by capitalists. No attempt will be made here to develop a so-called socialistic view of tourism because today's mass tourism at the international level is mainly associated with corporate tourism. In the thinking of many socialists, however, when those involved in promoting tourism become so obsessed with the material side of the industry, the real purpose of the activity is destroyed. This purpose might best be described as a social/psychological one: the use of leisure to renew one's spirit or as a just reward for one's labor.[1] The extravagance which accompanies American tourism in Third World countries, for example, adds more to the frustration of host peoples than to any kind of mutually rewarding experience for the visitor and host alike. These frustrations arise in part from the visibility of over-consumption and affluence which cannot readily be attained by the host residents. Socialists are inclined to say that whenever tourism becomes institutionalized by corporate capitalists, it becomes empty and purposeless at the least, and may well become exploitative and oppressive.

A clear challenge to this capitalistic view of tourism can be seen in the following statement by a former executive director of the Caribbean Travel Association, Herbert Hiller:

> We must recognize in tourism, therefore, the comprehensive reach of industrialization to encompass our leisure as well as our work. We are no more free of its influence when we are off-duty, so to speak, then we are on. And we are as determined by it, we people of the industrial society, as are the people of the former colonial world.
>
> Tourism is marketed today in response to assumptions of what it is the people of industrial society want. These assumptions are based on our wanting material goods. . . .
>
> The question becomes, is there some way that through the travel experience we might be able to satisfy our non-product-oriented needs.[2]

Hiller stresses the point that in destinations like the Caribbean a development mode for tourism might require that the industry be based more on non-industrial, non-material values in order to utilize local resources more efficiently. Where local resources are used, argues Hiller, a tourism geared to the high technology of the metropolitan states will prove useless as a contributor to national development. The assumptions of a straight capitalistic approach must be severely questioned.

Third World perceptions. — It is in the underdeveloped countries that the greatest ideological debate about tourism is taking place. In many Third World nations the intrusion of mass tourism from metropolitan centers has generated critical thoughts about the nature of international relations and about the effects of tourism upon host societies. In the Caribbean the ideological aspects of these observations tend to reflect four general views of tourism: (1) that the industry amounts to a new form of *colonialism* and *imperialism;* (2) that tourism is part of a new *plantation economy;* (3) that international mass tourism is rapidly selling much of the Third World as a *playground* for the industrial metropolitan pupulations, hence creating a synthetic playground culture; and (4) that much world tourism is an intrusion of white institutions and values into the non-white world.

Tourism as neo-colonialism and neo-imperialism. — Corporate capitalism and the rise of the multinational corporation have contributed greatly to the view of tourism as just a new form of colonialism and imperialism.[3] The intermingled foreign policies of metropolitan governments and their own corporations lead to suspicion within developing countries that corporate tourism has hidden motives. Profit is the apparent goal of the corporation. Political influence exercised through those companies by parent governments causes fears that tourism has become a means to political and economic domination of host countries. This influence often is interpreted as direct. That is, metropolitan diplomacy in host countries is highly focused upon the welfare of metropolitan business in those states. Consequently, the close interaction of diplomats and business executives is often termed imperialism by critics in the host society.

Under colonialism the legal and political relationships between the metropolitan mother state and its colonies were fairly clear. With the coming of independence to most colonies, the political and economic relations between the colony and the mother country were not immediately altered in spite of legal independence. Rather than the old method of exercising control through legal arrangements of authority, the metropolitan influence in the newly independent state now took the form of indirect economic control through business elites working in close contact with diplomats. Thus, to many Third World critics this colonialism in a new guise is the predominant feature of modern mass tourism. The industry serves primarily the interests of the metropolitan society just as actual colonialism did.

Charges of neo-imperialism are also common. Capitalistic countries seeking markets beyond their own borders have found tourism a convenient vehicle for foreign ventures. Lenin described imperialism as the final stage of capitalism, a stage at which local markets have been exhausted and new ones must be sought or created elsewhere.[4]

Metropolitan capitalistic countries try to dominate the foreign tourism market, especially in those areas where their own citizens travel most frequently. Air services, cruise lines, hotels, banks, and exported foods are all potential foreign markets related directly to tourism. When these markets are aggressively persued by metropolitan companies in conjunction with their governments' efforts, charges of imperialism tend to develop. It is not surprising, therefore, that at least a radical critique of tourism would include charges of neo-imperialism. Essential both to neo-colonialism and neo-imperialism is the manipulation and control of local elites by agents of metropolitan interests. Foreigners come to dominate or at least heavily influence decision-making in the host country. One scholar has written of foreign influence in the Caribbean, ". . . the decisions made conerning what is produced and how it is produced are those consistent with signals from home, not with those generated locally. . . . Not only are foreigners making the key decisions, but from the point of view of growth, usually they are making the wrong ones."[5] This kind of management and influence is usually effected through a combination of corporate skill and diplomatic finesse.

Tourism and plantation economics. — There is a contention in the Caribbean that tourism and other multinational businesses amount to a new type of plantation economy. This view is closely related to the critique of tourism as neo-colonialism, for it sees the whole thrust of tourism activity as being geared to meet the needs and demands of metropolitan societies. Further, like the old agricultural plantation under colonialism these new enterprises swiftly transfer accumulated wealth from the colony to the motherland. In Third World host countries the corporate institutions of tourism treat their servants with "benign neglect," flavored occasionally by injections of paternalistic concern. Plantation managers are usually recruited from the metropolitan centers, but lower level managers are selected from among the local elites in order to maintain contact with local labor.

George Beckford, a West Indian economist, has maintained that the central question about the plantation system is whether or not it has been responsible for the lack of lasting development in those societies where they have operated.[6] It is likely that tourism as a metropolitan intrusion into developing countries can be criticized in response to this question. Tourism may add to the numbers of jobs available and it may increase the trappings of modernity with modern buildings and new services, but if it does not contribute to the development of local resources, then it differs little from the traditional agricultural plantation. Wealth which is generated by the enterprise gets transferred back to the home base of the company.

Metropolitan tourism in Third World countries also seems to fit Lloyd Best's description of a *pure plantation economy* in that (1) tourism is structurally a part of an overseas economy; (2) it is held together by a system of law and order; and (3) there is little or no way to calculate the flow of values.[7] In other words, metropolitan institutions which invest in tourism in many different countries are able to manipulate their accounts in ways that are conducive to higher profit at the international level without the various host governments being able to detect it. Tourism, like the old plantation investments, is highly dependent upon local elites to maintain law and order. Expenditures on the social infrastructure of the plantation are determined by what it takes to keep the slaves happy and working or at least non-mutinous.

For those who see corporate tourism as a new plantation arrangement, perhaps the most crucial analogy lies in the account books of the *planters*. Host countries find it difficult to determine the true profit levels of expatriate firms or how profits are calculated

Tourism and the rise of playground culture. — There are also many Third World observers who see the effects of mass tourism more in cultural than in economic terms. Especially in sunspot destinations such as the Caribbean and the Pacific, the growth of tourism promotes a playground mentality among visitors and residents alike. Globally, these countries are seen as playgrounds for the affluent metropolitan residents who seek "far away places with strange-sounding names" in pursuit of exotic leisure. Because of the high visibility of tourism in some developing areas, the values and behavior of tourists who are on holiday become subtle but noticeable influences upon host peoples.

There are two rather important accusations within the playground scenario. One is the idea that metropolitan promoters of tourism and some tourists have come to view Third World destinations not as sovereign countries striving to preserve their culture and identity, but rather as socially uninhibited places where metropolitan visitors can "unwind" amid an abundance of sun, sea, sand and sex — the four s's.

A second accusation is that because of the pervasiveness of this playground attitude, local residents begin to view themselves as part of the holiday culture, thus abandoning their own values and traditions.

Turner and Ash have referred to the world's playgrounds as the *pleasure periphery*. (See footnote 14, Chapter 1.) Geographically, this periphery refers to a strip of the globe near the equator, including the Mediterranean region, the islands of the Indian and Pacific Oceans, Acapulco, Florida, and the Caribbean — the sunbelt or, as airline people like to say, the *sunspot destinations*. Whatever the appropriate labels might be, many critics of mass international tourism are alarmed at the seeming proliferation of the playground culture in the Third World. When considered along with criticisms of the economic thrusts of the neo-colonialism, this interpretation of tourism does raise some challenging questions about the future of world tourism — issues which must be dealt with firmly by host governments in developing nations.

Tourism as white intrusion. — Finally, so much of the Third World is racially non-white, while most tourists are white. This leads to the rise of racialistic views of tourism. Some thinkers who also subscribe to all of the above Third World perceptions of tourism stress the element of race.[8] In other words, these critics would object to much institutionalized tourism not only because it is organized and sold by capitalists, but more importantly because it is promoted by *white capitalists* for *white tourists*. Tourism has become just another method whereby white societies exploit non-white peoples.

Those who see tourism as white intrusion are not opposed to all tourism. They reject the features of the activity that others stress: that the economic rewards accrue mainly to external societies, and that foreign values and institutions are imposed upon the most societies. Yet, race becomes an obsessive dimension of tourism simply because black people continue to be the ones who are exploited by international commerce. Slavery in the Caribbean, for example, was at one time the essential base for colonialism. If one perceives that economic relations since colonialism have not changed fundamentally, then it must follow that modern mass tourism is propped up by cheap black labor in host countries. Throughout the transition from the slavery of the last century to the contemporary multinational businesses of the present time, the abundance of black labor has been exploited by white foreign intruders. World tourism, like sugar, bananas or cotton, becomes just another commodity to be exploited for profit.

Tourism as fantasy. — For anyone who has ever been a tourist, charges of neo-colonialism, imperialism, or capitalistic intrusion are not likely to be meaningful interpretations of foreign holidays. Rather, they are likely to be concepts remote to the minds of tourists and tourism promoters alike. But to be told that tourism is essentially an exercise in fantasy comes as a rude awakening and yet, as an easily understood indictment.

Tourism as fantasy is not so new as it is unpopular, especially among metropolitan pushers of distant pleasure. For both the tourists and the corporate capitalists alike, it is insulting to be told that most foreign holidays amount to interruptions in reality, that the metropolitan consumer seeks a vacation in a fantasy world and the industry strives to provide it.

The fantasies are several. From the beginning of a holiday most tourists expect conditions which surpass those of everyday life. The quality of food, beverage, entertainment, service and accommodations must exceed that which they personally possess at home. Moreover, the holiday and playground atmosphere must allow them to be less inhibited than they would be at home. There must be some familiar things such as American food or air conditioned hotel rooms with modern plumbing. Psychologically, the fantasy must include all of these in order that the tourist is both content and intrigued with his foreign experience. The fantasy includes also a commitment to total servility on the part of everyone except the tourists. This practice has become so expected that when it is denied, violent reaction can often be expected. Hotel and airline managers tend to agree that it is the low or moderate-income tourist who is most demanding while on holiday. It is they who scream at waiters or wear only their undergarments in the lobby of the Barbados Hilton. They have been sold the fantasy of tourism, but have difficulty sometimes in coping with it.

The fantasies of tourism are profitable. Corporate advertising not only helps create the dream but promises to make it all come true. The four *s's* are packaged, advertised, and marketed with seemingly great detachment from reality. Barbados is a land of beautiful beaches, clear blue water, and friendly black people with great white smiles. It *could not be* a small new country with a colonial and slave history which has many of the same social and economic problems found in the rest of the world. *It is an island paradise, waiting to be discovered by you.*

As we stressed in the previous chapter, the tourism fantasy includes an assumption that one's behavior in the host country will somehow be accepted, no matter what one does. A recent article in *Playboy* magazine, for example, described the eastern Caribbean as a place where one might go in the summer months to frolic without clothes. No word of caution to the reader was included to the effect that West Indians are conservative and religious people who would likely be offended by the behavior and by the photographs which accompanied the article. While most residents of the eastern Caribbean shall probably never see the article or the pictures, their publication in North America is symptomatic of the tourism playground fantasy. The *Playboy* concern for local culture was summed up in the following generous statement:

> Their up-for-grabs, blood-on-the-bougainvillea past is everywhere a presence, different on every island, visible in ruins of dead forts and sugar mills and plantation houses again becoming rock heaps among the coco palms — and felt as subtle vibrations from the people who live there and have inherited it all, whose anything-goes genealogies usually include whatever you'd care to name but nearly always spin back to slave or planter or ferocious Carib. Levels and levels, as we used to say in the good old psychedelic days, and you don't even need to be Melville to find them fascinating or to learn something from them — *and you can do it from poolside, while sipping a rum punch.* Can you beat metaphysics *and* a terrific tan? (first italics mine)[9]

Club Mediterranee has quickly become the most cited example of the institutionalized fantasy. An image has developed of the club which suggests that it is the place to go for uninhibited sex, lots of food, drink, and group recreation, all with little or no contact with the host population except for brief sexual encounters with the native club staff. As *Playboy* describes it:

> For sex, it's Club Mediteranee, hands down. . . . As for Club

Mediteranee, most of what you've heard about it is probably true, the good along with the bad. There are three club villages in the Caribbean . . . And, yes, two of them are sex factories.[10]

Sun, sea, sand, and sex, and servility (now the five *s*'s) are the essential ingredients of tropical tourism fantasy. To these can be added the notion that creature comforts are required: exotic food, drink, entertainment, comfortable quarters. Anyone who urges that mass tourism abandon these fantasies is usually thought of as weird, radical, or at best unknowledgeable of the real value of tourism.

The fantasy view of tourism has never had a more knowledgeable or articulate spokesman than Herbert Hiller. As a cruise line executive Hiller observed first hand the tourism fantasy. His efforts to amend the unreality of cruises began in 1970 and 1971 when he organized a people-to-people program for Norwegian Caribbean Lines operating out of Miami. The effort began with Jamaica and later included Haiti and the Bahamas. Generally, the program brought together visitors and Jamaican families, and it provided opportunities for first hand experience in intercultural relations both onboard the ship and in the island.

Hiller subsequently became the executive director of the Caribbean Travel Association (later to become the Caribbean Tourism Association) and has taught tourism seminars at Florida International University in Miami. He has been in demand for tourism meetings all over the world. His view of tourism as fantasy has developed over a lengthy period of close involvement with the industry in several different roles. His efforts to reform the industry have been the subject of scores of newspaper and magazine articles dealing with Caribbean tourism and with the travel business in general.

Perhaps what is most important about Hiller's concept of tourism is his contention that the fantasies keep tourism from becoming a positive force for development and social growth, both in the sending and in the receiving societies. Hiller would contend that, especially in the Caribbean, the greatest monument (and monstrosity) ever constructed on behalf of tourism fantasy is the luxury hotel. In a sense the large luxury hotel is the symbol of all that is wrong with modern mass tourism. These enterprises perpetuate the fantasies and inhibit the visitors' exposure to local culture. Hiller advocates small hotels, owned and operated by local people, as the best means of indigenizing tourism and promoting development.

If luxury hotels are the epitomy of tourism fantasies in host countries, then cruise ships must play a similar if not more exaggerated role on the high seas. One does not have to be a cruise line executive, as Hiller was, to observe the carefully planned unrealness on a Caribbean cruise. A West Indian bartender with whom I became friendly and who had been on cruise ships for many years put the whole matter into crystal clear language. After several days of friendly chats about the Caribbean and about life onboard the ship, we engaged in the following dialogue:

> AUTHOR: What about the crew? How would you describe their attitudes toward the staff?
> BARTENDER: Oh, they are polite, but they keep pretty much to themselves. They don't like you to mix with them.
> AUTHOR: How about the passengers? Are they interested in you?
> BARTENDER: Well, they most often are quite proper people, you know. They ask me where I'm from and so forth, but mostly they seem interested in what's happening on the ship. What time bingo starts or when we arrive in the next port.
> AUTHOR: Do they ask you about your island? Does the company try to inform them about the Caribbean or about certain countries?
> BARTENDER: Yes, but the passengers aren't really that interested. A few come up to the bar and talk to me about things, but I think the company must feel that if you just keep them full of food and drink, they won't cause you any problems. In fact, we sometimes joke about how much belching, farting and screwing goes on onboard.
> AUTHOR: I know what you mean. Yesterday, I think it was, I was offered six meals. Do you think passengers expect this?
> BARTENDER: Most of them do! But what the hell, so would I at that price!

On some cruises one can partake of as many as six to eight meals per day. Drinks are usually rather cheap in price and planned activities are available during most of the day. Missing is any serious attempt to put the passengers in touch with the cultures which to them represent only ports-of-call. As Hiller points out, the host countries are not seen as real places, only as stops along the way for shopping and a bit of sightseeing. The fantasy continues by land and by sea and by air.

Conclusion

Are these rather biased perceptions of transnational tourism meaningless, or are they worthy contributions to a better future world? Any studied concept of tourism is biased in the sense that the perceiver relies upon his own experiences and values in making judgments about the nature of the world around him. But without these different critiques of the same activity new generations of leaders and tourists cannot hope to forge a better, more harmonious society at any level.

The highly ideological views of tourism which have been discussed briefly here are honest beliefs held by real people. They are not mere debate topics useful at cocktail parties or at afternoon teas. Those who hold these theories are foremostly concerned with *what tourism is all about.* Can its role in international human affairs be exploited for the good? Or have we lost touch with the genuinely human needs around which tourism historically and philosophically was built? Has the whole affair become so institutionalized and impersonal that its cultural merits are irretrievably lost?

Many of the questions raised in this short chapter should lead one to be quite skeptical about the answers. Yet, some of tourism's most severe critics such as Herbert Hiller remain hopeful that a new day is coming — that with proper insight tourism can become *both* meaningful and profitable. Third World nations will have to make some hard decisions about the kind of societies they wish to have and tailor their foreign policies accordingly. Metropolitan consumers and their industry leaders will someday see the present quality of mass tourism, as demeaning of the tourist himself. When that occurs, hopefully the new day will be ushered in with marketing devices stressing the less material side of man's nature.

NOTES
Chapter 4

[1] See Robert W. MacIntosh, Tourism: Principles, Practices and Philosphies (Columbus, Ohio: Grid, Inc., 1972), p. 47.

[2] Herbert L. Hiller, "Integrating Tourism with Other Sectors Organized for Development — Agriculture and Industry," paper presented to the first conference on Caribbean Tourism sponsored by the Caribbean Tourist Research Center, Caracas, Venezuela, January 9-11, 1975.

[3] An excellent article summarizing these views is found in Louis A. Perez, Jr., "Tourism in the West Indies," *Journal of Communication,* vol. 25, no. 2 (Spring 1975), pp. 136-143.

[4] Nikolai Lenin, *Imperialism* (New York: Vanguard Press, 1929).

[5] Jay R. Mandle, "Neo-Imperialism: An Essay in Definition," *Social and Economic Issues,* vol. 16, no. 3 (September 1967), p. 320.

[6] See George L. Beckford, *Persistent Poverty* (New York: Oxford University Press, 1972), introduction.

[7] Lloyd Best, "A Model of Pure Plantation Economy," *Social and Economic Studies,* vol. 17, no. 3(September 1968), pp. 283-286.

[8] For a discussion of the white intrusion model, see Harry G. Matthews, *Multinational Corporations and Black Power* (Cambridge, Mass.: Schenkman Publishing Co., 1976).

[9] "The Best Kept Secret in the Caribbean or Thrills and Romance in the Leewards and Windwards," *Playboy* (May 1976), p. 102.

[10] *Ibid.,* p. 162-163. See also *Newsweek* (January 5, 1976), p. 44.

5
CONCLUSION: SYSTEM POLITICS AND TOURISM

Tourism is an amazing human activity. One can find within it the raw material for exhaustive field work by sociologists, psychologists, anthropologists, economists, political scientists and other scientists. The flight of our tourist-geese is at once a social, economic and political act. Some would even argue that such travel for pleasure is a theological endeavor.

Our concern here is with the political dimension of international tourism, but political acts frequently determine the other social qualities of tourism-related behavior in a given setting. They do this by imposing limits on the type and level of tourism activity. At the same time, however, governmental action may be the result of many things including non-political features of the tourism industry.

Tourism as an industry and as a human activity can be studied productively by all social and behavioral scientists (see Figure D). Knowledge about the sociological and psychological effects of mass tourism upon a host culture, for example, can become a significant input into political and governmental action. Subsequently, feedback from that political action can become a new influence upon other aspects of tourism such as economics. The literature of tourism today is fragmented from a social science perspective because there has been little effort to integrate the work of researchers in different fields. We have seen already how the salience of tourism as a political issue in a small country is tied to the social/psychological/economic perceptions of the effects of the industry upon people. Politics is also tied into the various ideological biases of persons who participate in the making of tourism policy. In this sense, tourism as a political issue cannot be separated from tourism as a larger social matter.

Sociologists have produced more studies of tourism related behavior than have other behavioral scientists, perhaps with the exception of economists. Sociologists have focused largely on groups —tourists, local residents, hotel employees, the police, and so forth —while anthropologists have raised questions about the effects of tourism upon man. Few tourism studies have appeared that are of a psychological nature, although there are many worth-

Figure D: Behavioral Science Dimensions of Tourism

Anthropology
Sociology
Psychology
Geography
Economics
Political Science

WORLD TOURISM
other related studies:
history
philosophy
theology
finance

Figure E: Political Relations in World Tourism

while investigations needed, especially by social psychologists. The inability of many hotel employees in Third World countries to adapt to luxury and affluence while living in poverty is an example. What does large scale tourism do to motivation or achievement of workers and residents in poverty-stricken destinations?

The geographers and the economists have begun admirable studies of tourism in many countries as have political scientists. All social scientists can draw upon the works of others and their numbers and productivity are growing. Professional meetings on tourism and the social sciences are now being held annually, especially in Europe and in the United States.

Let us move now to a summary of the politics of tourism. As an industry rising from man's efforts to meet certain needs, tourism sets into motion several important sets of political relations (see Figure E). First of all, both domestic and international tourism within a society create two clusters of domestic political relations; one which involves mainly private actors such as citizens or groups, and another which includes government and lobbyists. Examples of these political relations have been discussed in Chapter 2. The first set of domestic relations, is characterized by competing interests among various groups which seek gain from tourism, while the second set of relations is more directly an effort by these same groups to get government to aid in their pursuits through policy decisions. The relations can be harmonious; or they can contain significant conflict as when environmentalists object to the location of a new hotel, airport or other tourist facility. Such conflicts are all political in that they eventually require governmental action.

These sets of domestic political relations resulting from tourism can be found both in the metropolitan states and in the developing host countries where tourism is a viable issue. Essentially, they are domestic matters, but when they pertain to international tourism, additional political relations appear.

At least three different levels of international relations are generated by world tourism. First, at the non-governmental level private citizens of different countries come into contact and experience cultures different from their own. A kind of *private international relations* develop; these can, of course, be altered by governmental action.

A *public* level of international relations also results from tourism. Government-to-government dealings on matters essential to the industry form an important part of this level. The formation of world or regional tourism organizations is further evidence of this intergovernmental activity.

Today, however, the level of international relations most characteristic of world tourism is the involvement of private actors such as corporations (airlines, banks, hotels) with governments other than their own. Modern mass tourism is mainly corporate tourism, and its success is greatly dependent upon the ability to gain favorable treatment at the hands of governments, foreign and domestic. The outcomes of these kinds of relations, more than any single activity, determine the direction, costs, and frequncy of the flights of our tourist-geese.

A Systematic View of Tourism

World tourism politics might be seen in yet another meaningful light, that of systems analysis. It has been suggested that the politics of tourism is a process whereby the question of *who gets what* is settled. Public policy, or the lack of it, will most directly establish the gains and losses of many groups in tourisim.

In Figure F, a systems model of tourism politics is illustrated. Examples are offered of inputs into tourism policy from both the internal and external environments of the society which the system rules. Various policy output areas related to tourism are also listed, such as labor policy, investment incentives, and so forth.

Figure F conceptualizes what really takes place in a given political system. The various inputs (demands or supports) related to tourism are considered by policymakers and are converted into outputs (tourism policies). It should be stressed, however, that in many political systems the lack of appropriate tourism policies is more apparent than are specific regulations. And in some cases this is exactly what is desired by tourism interest groups. The lack of policy could enhance profits and/or cut costs.

The Future and Tourism Politics

With special reference to the concepts illustrated in Figures E and F, there are certain trends which cause concern for the future of world tourism. Perhaps the most obvious of these is the reality that tourism politics is heavily loaded in favor of growth, profit and corporate tourism in general. In both the United States and Barbados, for example, the voices of tourism expansion are numerous and ring loud and clear. Those who question either the kind or volume of tourism seem to speak in hushed whispers. In Washington, lawmakers and bureaucrats alike seem shocked when asked if they know of any interest groups or lobbyists who oppose tourism growth anywhere. Since tourism is a *clean* industry, everyone must be for it! Only intellectuals, clergymen and other ideologues ever question the role of tourism in human relations, and what do they know?

While it is easy to be facetious about tourism's social value, the continuation of this imbalance in tourism politics could present negative effects. Policymakers who hear only the virtues of tourism are not likely to discover its ill effects. The dominant pressures in

Figure F: Systems Model of Tourism Politics*

EXTERNAL ENVIRONMENT

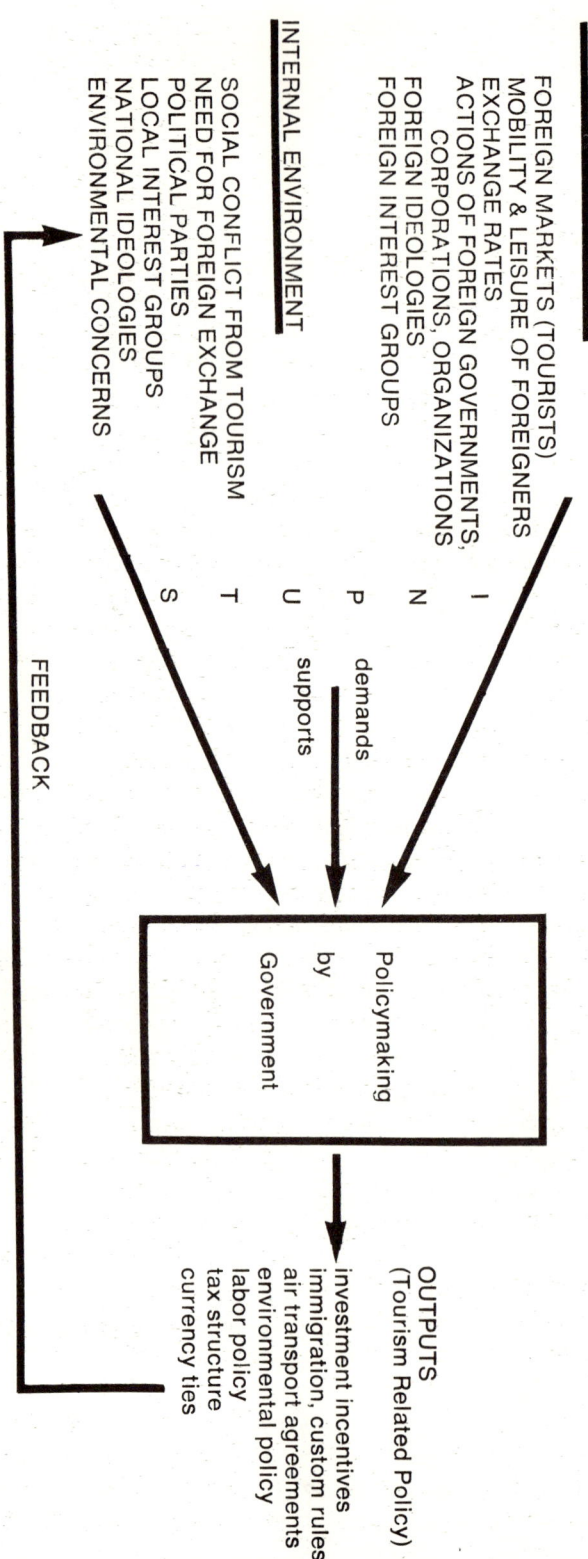

- FOREIGN MARKETS (TOURISTS)
- MOBILITY & LEISURE OF FOREIGNERS
- EXCHANGE RATES
- ACTIONS OF FOREIGN GOVERNMENTS, CORPORATIONS, ORGANIZATIONS
- FOREIGN IDEOLOGIES
- FOREIGN INTEREST GROUPS

INTERNAL ENVIRONMENT

- SOCIAL CONFLICT FROM TOURISM
- NEED FOR FOREIGN EXCHANGE
- POLITICAL PARTIES
- LOCAL INTEREST GROUPS
- NATIONAL IDEOLOGIES
- ENVIRONMENTAL CONCERNS

INPUTS
- demands
- supports

Policymaking by Government

OUTPUTS (Tourism Related Policy)
- investment incentives
- immigration, custom rules
- air transport agreements
- environmental policy
- labor policy
- tax structure
- currency ties

FEEDBACK

*Adapted from David Easton, *A Framework for Political Analysis* (Englewood Cliffs, New Jersey: Prentice Hall, 1965).

support of tourism are economic ones, while those which oppose certain aspects of the industry do so on more moralistic, cultural or philosophical basis. In Western capitalistic societies more attention has always been given in political circles to the *dollars and cents* approach.

The overbearing economic role of tourism has created another trend worthy of comment — namely, the depersonalization of the tourist and the tourist industry. While corporate domination of world tourism has made new destinations accessible, it has also packaged the tourist and, in a sense, sterilized him. It has minimized rather than maximized the inter-cultural experience of the consumer, and at an ever-rising price. Corporate leaders may conceivably find the future of mass tourism confined to conventions and special-interest itineraries.

Those few people who are today calling for the return of humanism to international tourism may have more insight and wisdom than do their critics. Their arguments are sound and reasonable, but their suggestions are not attractive to most corporate capitalists. Smaller hotels, more personalized service, and a touch of human relations are difficult to package. Hence, they are not a normal part of corporate theology.

Whatever may be the future nature of world tourism, we can be certain that a large part of it will be molded by the political behavior of people in their own communities as well as by political leaders at the national and international levels. The struggle for economic rewards continues to dominate the politics of tourism, and politics continues to be an exercise in *who gets what*.

SUGGESTED READINGS

Adams, John. "Why the American Tourist Abroad is Cheated," *Journal of Political Economy,* vol. 18 (January/February 1972), pp. 203-207.

Armstrong, W. E. et al. "Structural Analysis of the Barbados Economy, 1968, With an Application to the Tourist Industry," *Social and Economic Studies,* vol. 23 (December 1974), pp. 493-520.

Ball, D. A. "Permanent Tourism: A New Export Diversification for Less Developed Countries," *International Development Review,* no. 4 (1971), pp. 20-23.

Barbados, Central Bank of. *Economic and Financial Statistics,* published monthly.

Beckford, George L. *Persistent Poverty.* New York: Oxford University Press, 1972.

Best, Lloyd. "A Model of Pure Plantation Economy," *Social and Economic Studies,* vol. 17, no. 3 (September 1968), pp. 283-326.

Bryden, John M. *Tourism and Development: A Case Study of the Commonwealth Caribbean.* Cambridge: University Press, 1973.

Butler, R. W. "The Social Implications of Tourists Developments," *Annals of Tourism Research,* vol. 2, no. 2 (November/December 1974), pp. 100-111.

Christian Action for Development in the Eastern Caribbean. *The Role of Tourism in Caribbean Development.* Bridgetown, Barbados: CADEC, no date. (Conference report.)

Cohen, Erik. "Arab Boys and Tourist Girls in a Mixed Jewish-Arab Community," *International Journal of Comparative Sociology,* vol. 12, no. 4 (1971), pp. 217-233.

Cohen, Erik. "Nomads from Affluence: Notes on the Phenomenon of Drifter-Tourism," *International Journal of Comparative Sociology,* vol. 14, nos. 1 and 2 (1973), pp. 89-103.

Cohen, Erik. "Toward a Sociology of International Tourism," *Social Research,* vol. 39, no. 1 (1972), pp. 164-182.

Cohen, Erik. "Who is a Tourist? A Conceptual Clarification," *Social Research,* vol. 22 (November 1974), pp. 527-555.

Davis, H. David, "Potentials for Tourism in Developing Countries," *Finance and Development,* vol. 5 (December 1968), pp. 34-39.

Dolbeare, Kenneth and Dolbeare, Patricia. *American Ideologies,* 3rd ed. Chicago: Rand McNally, 1976.

Doxey, George V. and Associates. *The Tourist Industry in Barbados.* Kitchener, Ontario: Dusco Graphics Ltd., no date.

Evans, Nancy H. "Tourism and Cross Cultural Communication," *Annals of Tourism Research,* vol. 3, no. 4 (March/April 1976), pp. 189-198.

Fanon, Franz. *The Wretched of the Earth.* New York/London: Grove Press/Penquin, 1963.

Femina, Jerry D. *From those Wonderful Folks who Gave You Pearl Harbor.* London: Pan, 1972.

Field, James A., Jr., "Transnationalism and the New Tribe," *International Organization*, vol. 25, no. 3 (Summer 1971), pp. 353-372.
Forster, J. "The Sociological Consequences of Tourism," *International Journal of Comparative Sociology*, vol. 5, no. 2 (1964), pp. 217-227.
Francillon, G. "Tourism in Bali: Three Points of View. *International Social Science Journal*, no. 4 (1975), pp. 721-757.
Gray, H. Peter. *International Travel-International Trade*. Lexington, Mass.: Heath Lexington Books, 1970.
Gray, H. Peter. "Toward an Economic Analysis of Tourism Policy," *Social and Economic Studies*, vol. 23, no. 3 (September 1974), pp. 386-397.
Greenwood, Davydd J. "Tourism as an Agent of Change: A Spanish Basque Case," *Ethnology*, vol. 11 (January 1972), pp. 80-91.
Haden-Guest, Anthony. *Down the Programmed Rabbit Hole*. London: Hart-Davis, Macgibbon, 1972.
Harrigan, Norwell. "The Legacy of Caribbean History and Tourism," *Annals of Tourism Research*, vol. 2, no. 1 (September/October 1974), pp. 13-25.
Hiller, Herbert L. "The Development of Tourism in the Caribbean Region," *Air Travel and Tourism*. (August 1972.)
Inouye, Daniel K. "The United States Travel Service: An Example of the Federal Commitment to Tourism," *Annals of Tourism Research*, vol. 3, no. 5 (May/August 1976), pp. 248-258.
"International Tourism and Economic Development: A Special Case for Latin America," *Mississippi Valley Journal of Business and Economics*. (Fall 1972), pp. 43-45.
Koenig, Helmut. "Lifeseeing: Scandinavia's New Tourism," *Scandinavian Review*, no. 1 (1975), pp. 5-11.
Levitt, Kari and Gulati, Igbal. "Income Effects of Tourist Spending: Mystification Multiplied: A Critical Comment on the Zinder Report," *Social and Economic Studies*, vol. 19, no. 3 (September 1970), pp. 326-343.
Lundberg, Donald. *The Tourist Business*. Chicago: Institution/VFM Books, 1972.
MacCannell, Dean. *The Tourist*. New York: Schocken Books, 1976.
MacIntosh, Robert W. *Tourism: Principles, Practices and Philosophies*. Columbus, Ohio: Grid, Inc., 1972.
Mandle, Jay R. "Neo-Imperialism: An Essay in Definition," *Social and Economic Studies*, vol. 16, no. 3 (September 1967), p. 320.
Martyn, Howe, "International Tourism: Public Attitudes and Government Policies," *Dalhousie Review*, vol. 50 (Spring 1970), pp. 40-54.
Matthews, Harry G. *Multinational Corporations and Black Power*. Cambridge, Mass.: Schenkman, 1976.
National Tourism Resources Review Commission. *Destination U.S.A.* Washington: Gov't Printing Office, 1973. (6 vols.)
O'Connor, William E. *Economic Regulation of the World's Airlines*. New York: Praeger, 1971.
Organization for Economic Cooperation and Development, *Tourism and Tourism Policies in OECD Member Countries*. Paris: OECD, published annually.
Perez, Louis A., Jr. "Tourism in the West Indies," *Journal of Communication*, vol. 25, no. 2 (Spring 1975), pp. 136-143.
Peters, Michael. *International Tourism: The Economics and Development of the International Tourist Trade*. London: Hutchinson, 1969.

Pollard, H. J. "Tourism: The Growth Industry of the Caribbean," *Geography*, vol. 61 (April 1976), pp. 102-107.

Sessa, Alberto. "The Tourism Policy," *Annals of Tourism Research*, vol. 3, no. 5 (May/August 1976), pp. 234-247.

Smith, Valene L. "Tourism and Culture Change," *Annals of Tourism Research*, vol. 3, no. 3 (January/February 1976), pp. 122-126.

Sutton, W. A. "Travel and Understanding: Notes on the Social Structure of Touring," *International Journal of Comparative Sociology*, vol. 8, no. 2 (1967), pp. 218-223.

Thornton, Robert L. *International Airlines and Politics.* Ann Arbor: University of Michigan Press, 1970.

Turner, Louis and Ash, John. *The Golden Hordes.* London: Constable, 1975.

Turner, Louis. *Multinational Companies and the Third World.* London/New York: Allen Lane/Hill and Wang, 1974/1973.

United Nations Conference on Trade and Development. *Elements of Tourism Policy in Developing Countries.* New York: United Nations, 1973. (Sales no. E.73.II.D.3)

United States Travel Service. *Summary and Analysis of International Travel to the U.S.*, published periodically.

Wenkam, Robert. *The Great Pacific Rip Off.* Chicago: Follett Publishing Company, 1974.

Young, George. *Tourism: Blessing or Blight?* London: Penquin Books, 1973.

Zinder and Associates. *The Future of Tourism in the Eastern Caribbean.* Washington: Zinder and Associates, 1969.

EPILOGUE

Since international air transport is the most critical link in the process of world tourism, it seems appropriate to add a short postscript about recent events. In Chapter 2 the controversy over Laker Airways' proposal for a low-fare Skytrain operation between London and New York City was presented as continuing to be in limbo for the foreseeable future. In 1976 and 1977, however, the major issues which were holding back such an operation were resolved, and Laker commenced his service in September of 1977 with fares of 59 pounds from London to New York ($103.25) and $135 from New York to London.

In addition to Laker's troubles outlined in Chapter 2, his operating license issued in 1972 by the British Government was subsequently negated by the British Department of Trade. A British Court of Appeal in December 1976 ruled that the Department of Trade had acted illegally in revoking Laker's license and that, barring a government appeal to the House of Lords, Laker's rightful place as a designated British carrier on the New York-London route be restored.

The United States' position on the Laker affair had also been rather unclear. In 1974 an administrative law judge ruled that Laker Airways Ltd. met the qualifications of a scheduled carrier under the Bermuda Agreement with the United Kingdom, and that it should be granted permission to operate its low-fare service for an experimental period. The CAB made such a recommendation to President Carter on June 6, 1977, and the president signed it into effect on June 13 (Order 77-6-68).

In July 1977, the United States and the United Kingdom concluded a new air transport agreement under which Laker's Skytrain will operate as a British designated scheduled carrier along with British Airways serving London and New York.

Skytrain's first flight took place on September 26, 1977, about six years after Freddie Laker first put forth the idea. His battle with two governments cost him nearly $1 million, but it achieved at least one desired effect — to reduce transatlantic fares. Shortly after the CAB approved his operation, other transatlantic carriers immediately proposed comparable fares. Pan Am and TWA, both of whom opposed Laker's plan all along on the basis that his fares were not economically feasible, must now try to maintain control of those portions of their respective markets which they fear will go to Laker. In July, 1977, IATA's North Atlantic Traffic Conference met in Geneva to discuss ways of countering the new Laker fares. Ironically, on the same day that Skytrain commenced service (September 26, 1977), President Carter approved transatlantic fares for U.S. carriers that were only a few dollars higher than the Laker fare. In a sense, Laker had achieved his other major objective — a chance to risk his money in a *competitive* North Atlantic marketplace.

Why did the U.S. finally agree to Laker's desire to serve the London-New York route with such low fares, no frills, no reservations, and limited passenger loads?* There appear to be several reasons, but two seem most important. First of all, under the terms of the U.S.-United Kingdom bilateral agreements on air transport, each party is entitled to designate two carriers for each pair of cities — in this case London and New York. The British Government, even prior to its conflict in court with Laker, had designated Laker Airways as one of its two carriers. Under the agreement between the two governments, the United States had little choice but to accept Laker. Secondly, for the CAB, approval of the innovative service at the stated fare was in keeping with the belief that such a service is in the public interest, and that it is compatible with new Carter Administration policy that innovative low-fare experiments should be more common between the U.S. and foreign states.

In a sense, Skytrain was an idea whose time had come. In the United States the CAB had been accused by consumer groups of representing the interests of the airlines over the interests of the travelling public; and two presidents, Ford and Carter, had declared their belief that lower and more competitive fares at home and abroad were to be pursued by their government.

While lower transatlantic fares have become a reality, airline spokesmen doubt that the cost of flying to the Caribbean will be reduced in the near future. It is possible that lower transpacific fares, for example, might be a goal of the Carter administration in Washington. Such a trend toward lower international fares will have an impact on world tourism by making foreign destinations more accessible to metropolitan consumers.

---

*Laker's British license had a number of restrictions which were later revoked in 1977. A first he could operate one flight per day during October through April with a maximum of 89 seats per flight, and eleven flights per week during May through September with no more than 345 seats per flight. After IATA countered with cheap fares in 1977, Laker sought and got limitations on numbers of seats removed. Also, the British Government allowed him to operate from Gatwick airport rather than from Stanstead a move which was conducive to marketing and ground services.

In Chapter 2 there was some discussion of the relatedness of the Laker Skytrain proposal to the hopes of International Caribbean Airways to fly routes between Barbados and the United States. In March 1976, the CAB reviewed the application of ICA to fly two routes to the U.S.: one between Barbados and Boston with an intermediate stop in St. Lucia, and a second between Barbados and Washington, D.C., with intermediate stops in Antigua and St. Lucia. The Board left the matter open for discussion at a later date, but found that ICA was not "substantially owned and effectively controlled by nationals of Barbados or the Barbadian Government," and hence not really qualified to be designated by the Government of Barbados as a national carrier (see Order 76-3-116). In fact, said the CAB, the airline remains effectively controlled by Laker Airways even though the Barbados government *owns* 51% of the shares and appoints 4 of the 7 members of the board of trustees. (The airline leases its aircraft from Laker, who owns the other 49% of the shares.) There is no evidence that the Barbados government paid for its shares or that it has otherwise made a substantial financial commitment to the company. The CAB, unless it chooses to except a particular applicant, uses such criteria in making a decision to issue a foreign air carrier permit. ICA was invited by the CAB to re-negotiate its linkage with Laker and to re-apply for the permit. The CAB approval of Laker's Skytrain indicates that it is no longer Laker's personal involvement with ICA that matters, but rather a question of who really owns and operates the airline.